anxious

for

NOTHING

FINDING CALM *in a* CHAOTIC WORLD

BIBLE STUDY GUIDE | FIVE SESSIONS

MAX LUCADO

WITH JENNA LUCADO BISHOP

**Harper*Christian*
Resources**

Anxious for Nothing Bible Study Guide
© 2017, 2025 by Max Lucado

Published in Grand Rapids, Michigan, by HarperChristian Resources. HarperChristian Resources is a registered trademark of HarperCollins Christian Publishing, Inc.

Requests for information should be sent to customercare@harpercollins.com.

ISBN 978-0-310-14605-6 (softcover)
ISBN 978-0-310-14606-3 (ebook)

HarperChristian Resources titles may be purchased in bulk for church, business, fundraising, or ministry use. For information, please e-mail ResourceSpecialist@ChurchSource.com.

Published in association with Anvil II Management, Inc.

First Printing March 2025 / Printed in the United States of America

CONTENTS

A NOTE FROM MAX

Anxiety is a meteor shower of what-ifs. A trepidation. A suspicion. An apprehension. It's living life in a minor key with major concerns. You're part Chicken Little and part Eeyore. The sky is falling, and it's falling disproportionately on you.

Ever been tossed and turned by anxiety? If so, you aren't alone. According to the National Institute of Mental Health, anxiety disorders are reaching epidemic proportions. In a given year, nearly fifty million Americans will feel the effects of a panic attack, phobias, or other anxiety disorders.

The Bible is the most highlighted book on Kindle. And Philippians 4:6–7 is the most highlighted passage.[1] Why? Read these verses (and the ones on either side), and you will probably understand its appeal:

> [4] Rejoice in the Lord always. I will say it again: Rejoice! [5] Let your gentleness be evident to all. The Lord is near. [6] Do not be anxious about anything, but in every situation, by prayer and petition, with thanksgiving, present your requests to God. [7] And the peace of God, which transcends all understanding, will guard your hearts and your minds in Christ Jesus.
>
> [8] Finally, brothers and sisters, whatever is true, whatever is noble, whatever is right, whatever is pure, whatever is lovely, whatever is admirable—if anything is excellent or praiseworthy—think about such things.

The most highlighted Scripture promises something our anxious world craves: *peace*. Throughout this study, we will talk about how to live in this promise of God's supernatural peace. You and your group will walk through five sessions, each one dedicated to helping you find freedom from anxiety. You will learn what it looks like to rejoice in the Lord, how to exude a spirit of gentleness, and how to give all your worries to God. You will study the beautiful way God guards your heart and mind with his peace. And, finally, you will be challenged to examine your personal thought patterns and do what Paul charges you to do in Philippians 4:8: meditate on the things of God.

—MAX LUCADO

HOW TO USE THIS GUIDE

Need some more peace in your life? A bit less fret and a bit more faith? A heart not weighed down with fear? Then you are in the right place.

The *Anxious for Nothing* Bible study has been designed to help you take a closer look at the worries in your life, bring them before God, and receive his perfect and lasting peace. Before you begin, know that there are a few ways you can go through this material. You can experience this study with others in a group (such as a Bible study, Sunday school class, or other gathering), or you can go through the content on your own. Either way, the videos are available to view at any time by following the instructions provided with this study guide.

GROUP STUDY

Each of the sessions in this study are divided into two parts: (1) a group study section, and (2) a personal study section. The group study section provides a basic framework for how to open your time together, get the most out of the video content, and discuss the key ideas that were presented in the teaching. Each session includes the following:

- **Welcome:** A short opening note about the topic of the session for you to read on your own before you meet as a group.
- **Connect:** A few icebreaker questions to get you and your group members thinking about the topic and interacting with each other.
- **Read:** A short passage from the Bible for you and your group members to review and discuss before the video teaching.

- **Watch:** An outline of the key points covered in each video teaching along with space for you to take notes as you watch each session.
- **Discuss:** Questions to help you and your group reflect on the teaching material presented and apply it to your lives.
- **Respond:** A short personal exercise to help reinforce the key ideas.
- **Pray:** A few prompts to help you pray together and close out the group time.

If you are doing this study in a group, make sure you have your own copy of the study guide so you can write down your thoughts, responses, and reflections in the space provided—and so you have access to the videos via streaming. You will also want to have a copy of the *Anxious for Nothing* book, as reading it alongside this guide will provide you with deeper insights. (See the notes at the beginning of each group session and personal study section on which chapters of the book you should read before the next group session.)

Finally, keep these points in mind:

- **Facilitation:** If you are doing this study in a group, you will want to appoint someone to serve as a facilitator. This person will be responsible for starting the video and keeping track of time during discussions and activities. If *you* have been chosen for this role, there are some resources in the back of this guide that can help you lead your group through the study.

- **Faithfulness:** Your group is a place where tremendous growth can happen as you reflect on the Bible, ask questions, and learn what God is doing in other people's lives. For this reason, be fully committed and attend each session so you can build trust and rapport with the other members.

- **Friendship:** The goal of any small group is to serve as a place where people can share, learn about God, and build friendships. So seek to make your group a "safe place." Be honest about your thoughts and feelings, but also listen carefully to everyone else's thoughts, feelings, and opinions. Keep anything personal that your group members share in confidence so that you can create a community where people can heal, be challenged, and grow spiritually.

If you are going through this study on your own, read the opening Welcome section and reflect on the questions in the Connect and Read sections. Watch the video and use the outline to take notes. Finally, personalize the questions and exercises in the Discuss and Respond sections. Close by recording any requests you want to pray about during the week.

PERSONAL STUDY

In between your group times, you can maximize the impact of the course by checking out the C.A.L.M. personal study activities. This personal study (for you to do on your own) will help you reflect and actively respond to the lesson by practicing the acronym C.A.L.M.:

Celebrate God's Goodness
Ask God for Help
Leave Your Concerns with God
Meditate on Good Things

For each session, you may wish to complete the personal study in one sitting or spread it over a few days (for example, working on it a half-hour per day on four different days that week). Note that if you are unable to finish (or even start!) your between-sessions personal study, you should still attend the group time. Be assured that you are still wanted and welcome at the group even if you don't have your "homework" done.

There are plenty of things in this world that can cause you to worry. However, the goal is that after you go through this study—with God as your helper—you will sleep better, smile more, and reframe the way you face your fears. This course will give you practical tools to help you learn how to talk yourself off the ledge, view bad news through the lens of God's sovereignty, discern the lies of Satan, tell yourself the truth . . . and ultimately, start to lead a life characterized not by the daily chaos of your world but by *calm*.

Note: If you are a group leader, there are additional instructions and resources in the back of this guide to help you lead your group members through the study. Some of the activities require materials and setup, so be sure to read that section ahead of time so you will be prepared for each week's closing exercise.

WEEK 1

BEFORE GROUP MEETING	Read chapters 1–3 in *Anxious for Nothing* Read the Welcome section (page 2)
GROUP MEETING	Discuss the Connect questions Read the passage for this session and discuss Watch the video teaching for session 1 Discuss the questions that follow as a group Do the closing exercise and pray (pages 3–9)
STUDY 1	Complete the personal study (pages 13–15)
STUDY 2	Complete the personal study (pages 16–19)
STUDY 3	Complete the personal study (pages 20–21)
STUDY 4	Complete the personal study (page 22)
CATCH UP AND READ AHEAD (BEFORE WEEK 2 GROUP MEETING)	Read chapters 4–5 in *Anxious for Nothing* Complete any unfinished personal studies (page 23)

REJOICE *in the* LORD ALWAYS

We can't run the world, but we can entrust it to God. Peace is within reach, not for lack of problems, but for the presence of a sovereign Lord. Rather than rehearse the chaos of the world, we can choose to rejoice in the Lord's sovereignty.

MAX LUCADO

WELCOME [read on your own]

When I (Jenna) was growing up, my dad had school drop-off duty. And without fail, every morning as he slowed the car to a stop and we hurriedly unbuckled our seat belts, grabbed our backpacks, and threw open the doors, he would give the same exhortation: "Girls, have a good day. Laugh a lot. Learn a lot. And don't forget who gave it to ya."

I never thought much about the phrase growing up. My sisters and I would just robotically say it with him and then quickly yell, "Okay, Dad!" before slamming the car doors shut. Laugh, learn, remember. As a young girl I naturally did just that. Laughing came easily. Learning was fun. Remembering God as the giver of my day? It wasn't always on my mind, but I never doubted God was with me and cared for me.

But then I started to grow up. And with growing up came more responsibility. And with more responsibility came anxiety. It wasn't long before homework hours lengthened, friends hurt me, and I hurt them. Pretty soon I was taking my SATs, learning how to interview for jobs, paying bills. Marriage brought deep joy, but also deep struggles. Cancer invaded the family, and my heroes in life passed away. Babies were born—yet another level of worry.

The older I got, the less I naturally lived my dad's exhortation to laugh, learn, and remember. The serious struggles of life squelched laughter. The joy of learning turned into pressure to achieve. And remembering God? The anxieties of life pushed out thoughts of him.

That's why it's hard for me to accept Paul's words in Philippians 4:4, "Rejoice in the Lord always." *Always?* How are we supposed to do that with the pain and anxiety of life? In this session, we will see that rejoicing in the Lord does not mean we are in a constant state of excitement. We don't have to carry a guitar around and sing worship songs all day. It's not about plastering on a fake smile as we walk through a dark time. No, rejoicing in the Lord *always* is about a deep remembering.

Remembering that the Lord is here, *always*.

Remembering that the Lord is in control, *always*.

Remembering that the Lord is not only the giver of your day but also the ordainer of every minute inside of it, *always*.

Remembering that amidst the pressures, pain, and anxiety in life, he is sovereign, *always*.

As we remember, I have an inkling we may discover the carefree child we used to be. Laughing a lot more. Learning a lot more. And not forgetting who is with us through it all.

CONNECT [10 minutes]

If you or any of your group members don't know each other, take a few minutes to introduce yourselves. Then discuss one or both of the following questions:

· What interested you about this study? What do you hope to learn, and how do you hope to change because of it?

    — or —

· Describe someone in your life who embodies what it means to "rejoice in the Lord always." What does that person do or say to exude a heart with this attitude?

READ [15 minutes]

Ask someone to read Philippians 4:4–8 aloud for the group. This will be the theme passage for the next five sessions, so try to look at these words with new eyes and an open heart. Then read it again silently, circling or underlining words that stand out to you.

> [4] Rejoice in the Lord always. I will say it again: Rejoice! [5] Let your gentleness be evident to all. The Lord is near. [6] Do not be anxious about anything, but in every situation, by prayer and petition, with thanksgiving, present your requests to God. [7] And the peace of God, which transcends all understanding, will guard your hearts and your minds in Christ Jesus. [8] Finally, brothers and sisters, whatever is true, whatever is noble, whatever is right, whatever is pure, whatever is lovely, whatever is admirable—if anything is excellent or praiseworthy—think about such things.

Turn to the person next to you and take turns sharing your answers to the following questions:

· What was one thing that stood out to you from the passage?
· Why do these words stand out to you—and what fresh insight do they bring?
· What does "rejoicing in the Lord" mean? In your life, have you found it difficult or natural to rejoice in the Lord? Why?

WATCH [25 minutes]

Watch the video for this session, which you can access by playing the DVD or through streaming (see the instructions provided with this guide). As you watch, use the following outline to record any key thoughts or concepts that stand out to you.

Anxiety is not so much the onslaught of a storm as the continual threat that one is coming. It's a big heap of what-ifs.

The word *anxiety* actually comes from a Latin root that means "to choke" or "to squeeze." Its strong grip interrupts your sleep, chokes your energy, and harms your overall well-being.

Anxiety is a close cousin to fear, but the two are not twins. Fear *sees* a threat, while anxiety *imagines* one.

We have been taught the Christian life is one of peace. When we don't have peace, we assume the problem is within us, which leads us to feel guilty. But while the *presence* of anxiety is unavoidable, the *prison* of anxiety is optional.

When Paul writes to "be anxious for nothing," he is referring to an ongoing state. His words could be translated, "Don't let anything in life leave you *perpetually* in angst and breathless."

Paul's prescription for anxiety is a call to "rejoice in the Lord." This is not a call to a *feeling* but to a *decision*.

The sovereignty of God refers to his perfect governing over all things. God works in and through every detail of his creation to accomplish his divine purpose. We have the astounding privilege to be a part of this perfect plan.

To rejoice in the Lord, we must have a deep belief in his sovereignty over our lives. The more we believe in *his* control, the more we relinquish *our* control.

DISCUSS [40 minutes]

Discuss what you just watched by answering the following questions.

1. Stress-related ailments cost the United States billions of dollars every year. Why do you think the nation leading much of the world in infrastructure, education, democracy, and more is also leading the world in anxiety? Why would Americans suffer from anxiety more than people of lesser developed countries?

2. Scripture includes many verses that can bring comfort and peace to the worried heart. Read Psalm 56:3, Matthew 6:25–34, and 1 Peter 5:6–8. What prescription does each passage give for anxiety?

3. How does the world teach us to cope with anxiety? How does the world's solution for anxiety differ from God's solution?

4. Eugene Peterson says, "[The fact] that God followers don't get preferential treatment in life always comes as a surprise."[2] Have you ever expected special treatment from God? If so, how did it affect your relationship with him when you experienced hard times?

5. Read 2 Corinthians 12:1–10, where Paul talks about a constant trial God would not take away. What is God's response to Paul's prayer in verse 9? How does God display his strength when we are feeling weak or anxious?

6. The first prescription Paul gives for anxiety is this: "Rejoice in the Lord always." Hundreds of years before Paul wrote his letter, the prophet Habakkuk wrote similar words. Read Habakkuk 3:17–19. How does Habakkuk describe God in these verses? Why does Habakkuk say he can rejoice in God though the fig trees wither and crops fail?

7. If you want to rejoice in God regardless of your circumstances, it is crucial that you learn to trust in his sovereignty. What prevents you from trusting in the sovereignty of God?

8. How does trusting in God's sovereignty affect the way you perceive life's trials?

RESPOND [15 minutes]

(For this activity, each participant will need a sheet of paper, a pen, and an envelope.) In today's session, Max described the difference between fear and anxiety. Fear sees a threat, while anxiety imagines one. Fear screams, "Get out!" Anxiety ponders, "What if?" Take a minute to write down three what-ifs that are causing you anxiety—three worries that are weighing you down. Once you are finished, fold up the piece of paper and tuck it away in the envelope. Write your name on the outside of the envelope and give it to your group leader. At the end of this study, he or she will pass out the individual envelopes so you can reevaluate the list and see how God has brought supernatural peace to these anxious places in your heart.

PRAY [15 minutes]

Wrap up this time by talking to your heavenly Father. Your group may want to begin the prayer time by reading aloud Isaiah 45:9–12, a powerful passage about the sovereignty of God:

> [9] Woe to those who quarrel with their Maker,
>   those who are nothing but potsherds
>   among the potsherds on the ground.
> Does the clay say to the potter,
>   "What are you making?"
> Does your work say,
>   "The potter has no hands"?
> [10] Woe to the one who says to a father,
>   "What have you begotten?"
> or to a mother,
>   "What have you brought to birth?"
> [11] This is what the LORD says—
>   The Holy One of Israel, and its Maker:
> Concerning things to come,
>   do you question me about my children,
>   or give me orders about the work of my hands?

> [12] It is I who made the earth
> and created mankind on it.
> My own hands stretched out the heavens;
> I marshaled their starry hosts.

Now take some time to pray for one another. Split into groups of two or three or circle up and pray for the person next to you. Here are a few suggestions of ways to pray:

- Ask the Lord to give you a deeper trust in his sovereignty so you can rejoice in him no matter what circumstances come your way.
- Use the passage you just read in Isaiah 45:9–12 and declare its promises and/or truth over the person you are praying for. (Insert the person's name into the verse, or simply ask that the truth of this verse would be true in his or her life.)
- Ask the Lord to overwhelm the anxious thoughts you each wrote down earlier with the supernatural peace he promises in Philippians 4:7.

PERSONAL STUDY

As you discovered in this session, the goal of this study is to help you and your fellow group members find freedom from anxiety by working through Paul's prescription for peace found in Philippians 4:4–8. To this end, the personal study portion of each session will help you reflect on the content you've covered during the teaching so you can better apply it to your life. Each personal study section will consist of the following C.A.L.M. activities:

C *Celebrate God's Goodness* (Philippians 4:4): This will be a time to rejoice in the Lord, praising him for his goodness and for the new insight he is giving you through this study. Celebrating what God is teaching you and meditating on who God is will help shift your gaze from the problems on earth to your hope in heaven.

A *Ask God for Help* (Philippians 4:6): During this reflection time, you will ask God to help you not only understand what he is teaching you through the lesson but also to supernaturally transform your heart to live out this truth in your daily life.

L *Leave Your Concerns with God* (Philippians 4:7): This reflection activity will challenge you to leave your worries in the hands of God and pick up the specific worry weapons you are learning in each video session. That way, when worries threaten to return, you can fight them.

M *Meditate on Good Things* (Philippians 4:8): At the end of Paul's prescription against anxiety, he urges his readers to meditate on things that are of God.

In this activity, you will meditate on Philippians 4:4–8 and memorize a portion of it. In this way you will take the first step to replace anxious thoughts with the truth of God's Word.

The time you invest will be well spent, so let God use it to draw you closer to him. At your next meeting, you will have a few minutes to share with your group any key points or insights that stood out to you as you spent this time with the Lord. Before you begin, if you are reading *Anxious for Nothing* alongside this study, first review chapters 1–3 in the book.

CELEBRATE GOD'S GOODNESS

During this week's group time, you learned why it is important to always rejoice in the Lord. Put the lesson into practice today by reading Psalm 145:8–20, a passage that celebrates the goodness of God. If you are in a setting that lends itself to doing so, read the verses aloud. This is not only a time of reflection but also a time of worship!

> [8] The LORD is gracious and compassionate,
>   slow to anger and rich in love.
> [9] The LORD is good to all;
>   he has compassion on all he has made.
> [10] All your works praise you, LORD;
>   your faithful people extol you.
> [11] They tell of the glory of your kingdom
>   and speak of your might,
> [12] so that all people may know of your mighty acts
>   and the glorious splendor of your kingdom.
> [13] Your kingdom is an everlasting kingdom,
>   and your dominion endures through all generations.
>
> The LORD is trustworthy in all he promises
>   and faithful in all he does.
> [14] The LORD upholds all who fall
>   and lifts up all who are bowed down.
> [15] The eyes of all look to you,
>   and you give them their food at the proper time.
> [16] You open your hand
>   and satisfy the desires of every living thing.

> [17] The LORD is righteous in all his ways
>   and faithful in all he does.
> [18] The LORD is near to all who call on him,
>   to all who call on him in truth.
> [19] He fulfills the desires of those who fear him;
>   he hears their cry and saves them.
> [20] The LORD watches over all who love him,
>   but all the wicked he will destroy.

1. Look back at the passage and underline all the character attributes of God. Which one of these attributes do you have the hardest time trusting?

2. Why do you think you have a harder time trusting this particular characteristic of God's heart?

3. What description of God in this passage brings you the most comfort today? Why does it bring you comfort in this season of your life?

PRAY

Take some time to celebrate God's goodness by thanking him for the specific character trait you just wrote about. You might pray words to this effect:

Thank you, God, for your _____. Help me not only to remember your goodness on a daily basis but also to trust in it. May the goodness of you bring out your goodness in me. Amen.

Don't drown in the bilge of your own condemnation. There is a reason the windshield is bigger than the rearview mirror. Your future matters more than your past. God's grace is greater than your sin. What you did was not good. But your God is good. And he will forgive you. He is ready to write a new chapter in your life. Say with Paul, "Forgetting the past and looking forward to what lies ahead, I strain to reach the end of the race and receive the prize for which God is calling us" (Philippians 3:13–14 TLB).[3]

ASK GOD *for* HELP

It is one thing to accept in your mind that you should *rejoice in the Lord always* but quite a different matter when it comes to actually putting that into practice. So, before you begin this study, think about what it is in your life that tends to prevent you from rejoicing in the Lord always—whether that is a situation, a person, or anything else. Take a minute to examine your heart and then write down your thoughts. Be specific!

Now read the following passage from Luke 1:26–55 and answer the questions that follow.

[26] In the sixth month of Elizabeth's pregnancy, God sent the angel Gabriel to Nazareth, a town in Galilee, [27] to a virgin pledged to be married to a man named Joseph, a descendant of David. The virgin's name was Mary. [28] The angel went to her and said, "Greetings, you who are highly favored! The Lord is with you."

[29] Mary was greatly troubled at his words and wondered what kind of greeting this might be. [30] But the angel said to her, "Do not be afraid, Mary; you have found favor with God. [31] You will conceive and give birth to a son, and you are to call him Jesus. [32] He will be great and will be called the Son of the Most High. The Lord God will give him the throne of his father David, [33] and he will reign over Jacob's descendants forever; his kingdom will never end."

[34] "How will this be," Mary asked the angel, "since I am a virgin?"

[35] The angel answered, "The Holy Spirit will come on you, and the power of the Most High will overshadow you. So the holy one to be born will be called the Son of God. [36] Even Elizabeth your relative is going to have a child in her old age, and she who was said to be unable to conceive is in her sixth month. [37] For no word from God will ever fail."

[38] "I am the Lord's servant," Mary answered. "May your word to me be fulfilled." Then the angel left her.

[39] At that time Mary got ready and hurried to a town in the hill country of Judea, [40] where she entered Zechariah's home and greeted Elizabeth. [41] When Elizabeth heard Mary's greeting, the baby leaped in her womb, and Elizabeth was filled with the Holy Spirit. [42] In a loud voice she exclaimed: "Blessed are you among women, and blessed is the child you will bear! [43] But why am I so favored, that the mother of my Lord should come to me? [44] As soon as the sound of your greeting reached my ears, the baby in my womb leaped for joy. [45] Blessed is she who has believed that the Lord would fulfill his promises to her!"

[46] And Mary said:

> "My soul glorifies the Lord
> [47] and my spirit rejoices in God my Savior,
> [48] for he has been mindful
> of the humble state of his servant.
> From now on all generations will call me blessed,
> [49] for the Mighty One has done great things for me—
> holy is his name.
> [50] His mercy extends to those who fear him,
> from generation to generation.
> [51] He has performed mighty deeds with his arm;
> he has scattered those who are proud in their inmost thoughts.
> [52] He has brought down rulers from their thrones
> but has lifted up the humble.
> [53] He has filled the hungry with good things
> but has sent the rich away empty.
> [54] He has helped his servant Israel,
> remembering to be merciful
> [55] to Abraham and his descendants forever,
> just as he promised our ancestors."

1. What fears or anxious thoughts could have flooded Mary's mind when she received the angel's message?

2. Instead of stewing in anxiety, how did Mary respond (see verse 38)?

3. How did Mary's posture of servanthood enable her to rejoice in the Lord?

4. When we see ourselves as God's servants instead of God's advisors, we are in a much better position to trust in his sovereignty. Through Mary's story, we can infer that one of the biggest hindrances to rejoicing in the Lord is a failure to submit to his authority over our lives. Mary could freely rejoice because she could humbly submit, and her rejoicing overflowed into a song of worship (see verses 46–55). Look at the song again. In verse 47, why does Mary say her spirit rejoices in the Lord?

PRAY

Ask the Lord to specifically help you rejoice in him the way Mary rejoiced in him. Ask him to help you submit to his sovereignty. And finally, ask the Lord to help you deeply believe in Mary's words found in verse 48—that he is mindful of you. He sees your worries and is with you through it all. What a beautiful reason to rejoice!

> You can't run the world, but you can entrust it to God. This is the message behind Paul's admonition to "rejoice in the Lord." Peace is within reach, not for lack of problems, but because of the presence of a sovereign Lord. Rather than rehearse the chaos of the world, rejoice in the Lord's sovereignty, as Paul did. "The things which happened to me have actually turned out for the furtherance of the gospel, so that it has become evident to the whole palace guard, and to all the rest, that my chains are in Christ" (Philippians 1:12–13 NKJV).[4]

LEAVE YOUR CONCERNS *with* GOD

In this session, we have been discussing a powerful tool to fight anxiety: *rejoicing in the Lord.* When we do this, it changes our perspective, shrinks the anxiety, and magnifies God's glory. What specific concerns are clouding your thoughts these days? Write them in the "Worries" column below. This is a time to get what's on the inside on the outside, to let God's light shine on the darkness that's weighing on your heart. When you are finished, move to the "Worship" column. Next to each worry you wrote, write a reason you have to rejoice in the Lord. (You may want to refer to the Psalm 145 passage used in the first activity.)

WORRIES	WORSHIP

TAKE ACTION!

Take this activity a step further by encouraging a friend with what you are learning. Text, call, and/or email a friend in your group or any friend on your mind. Ask the friend to share a worry you can pray for, and then assure that person of God's goodness, perhaps using a verse you have read during this study or just a simple reminder that God is sovereign over his or her life. Rejoicing in the Lord is even more meaningful when shared!

> We have a choice. We can wear our hurt or wear our hope. We can outfit ourselves in our misfortune, or we can clothe ourselves in God's providence. We can cave in to the pandemonium of life, or we can lean into the perfect plan of God. And we can believe this promise: "In all things God works for the good of those who love him, who have been called according to his purpose" (Romans 8:28).[5]

MEDITATE *on* GOOD THINGS

Open your Bible and study Philippians 4:4—"Rejoice in the Lord always. I will say it again: Rejoice!"—until you can recite it from memory. Don't forget to memorize the verse reference as well. In case you need some help, here are a few memorization techniques:

- Write down the verse multiple times.
- Say the verse aloud multiple times.
- Break up the verse into smaller parts and memorize one section at a time.
- Write down the verse on note cards and place them where you will see them often—your bathroom mirror, your refrigerator, your computer, your car.

After you've reviewed this verse several times, write it down from memory in the space below. As an added challenge, in the upcoming weeks you will be asked to add to what you've memorized until you can say all of Philippians 4:4–8 by heart.

Close by asking the Lord to bring this verse to mind any time an anxious thought surfaces.

CATCH UP *and* READ AHEAD

Use this time to go back and complete any of the study and reflection questions from previous studies that you weren't able to finish. Make a note below of any questions you've had and reflect on any growth or personal insights you've gained.

Read chapters 4–5 in *Anxious for Nothing* before the next group gathering. Use the space below to make note of anything in those chapters that stands out to you or encourages you.

WEEK 2

BEFORE GROUP MEETING	Read chapters 4–5 in *Anxious for Nothing* Read the Welcome section (page 26)
GROUP MEETING	Discuss the Connect questions Read the passage for this session and discuss Watch the video teaching for session 2 Discuss the questions that follow as a group Do the closing exercise and pray (pages 26–33)
STUDY 1	Complete the personal study (pages 36–38)
STUDY 2	Complete the personal study (pages 39–44)
STUDY 3	Complete the personal study (pages 45–47)
STUDY 4	Complete the personal study (page 48)
CATCH UP AND READ AHEAD (BEFORE WEEK 3 GROUP MEETING)	Read chapters 6–7 in *Anxious for Nothing* Complete any unfinished personal studies (page 49)

LET YOUR GENTLENESS *be* EVIDENT *to* ALL

When the storms of life are raging and the ship is breaking apart, the others on board may freak out, but the gentle person is sober-minded and clear-thinking. Like Paul, they look to God for the solution and remain contagiously calm. The contagiously calm person is the one who reminds others that God is in control.

MAX LUCADO

WELCOME [read on your own]

Not too long after my daughter was born, I (Jenna) reached out to my cousin Dana for parenting advice. With four kids all grown and out of the house, she had years of parenting experience. I had *days*. I was desperate for her wisdom.

She sent me an email listing morsels of wisdom that I quickly gobbled up. She told me to be silly, get dirty, and play dress-up. She told me to pray, pray, pray. She told me to sleep anytime I could and spend quality, uninterrupted time with my daughter.

And then there was this one: *Find your poker face.* When my daughter falls down and hurts herself, she will cry a lot less if I respond with a calm face rather than one that shows fear. Fast-forward fifteen years. She may walk in the door, tears running down her face, confessing something I thought my innocent baby girl could never do. If I respond with calmness, she may share more. But if I react in fear, she may retract.

Find your poker face and practice it, Dana wrote.

I have to admit I was once that fifteen-year-old girl, confessing something my parents never imagined I would do. And I'll never forget my dad's response. He didn't react with yelling or instant punishment. Instead, he calmly held me as I cried. He reassured me of his love for me. And then he did something interesting. He told me to promise him that if I ever found myself in a similar situation again, to call him and he would come and pick me up. Dad knew the trial would probably resurface, and when it did, he wanted to be with me.

The calmness of my dad's response was contagious. My fifteen-year-old self calmed down. I knew I could share anything with him and still be loved.

We have a heavenly Father who is with us through every trial. And he invites you and me to talk to him about each one. So the next time you look into the face of a problem, look into the face of your Father. He will never react with impatience or condemnation. Only gentleness.

CONNECT [10 minutes]

If you or any of your group members don't know each other, take a few minutes to introduce yourselves. Then discuss one or both of the following questions:

- Think of someone in your life who is contagiously calm. How does that person display gentleness even during tense times?

    —or—

- What challenge is testing your gentleness right now? What strategies have you used to stay calm during this challenge? Have they worked?

If time permits, discuss the following questions related to the last session:

- Last time, we discussed Paul's first prescription for anxiety: *rejoicing in the Lord always*. How has this antidote brought you more peace since the last time your group met?
- If you participated in the C.A.L.M. personal study, what were some things you learned about yourself? Maybe you engaged in the "Take Action!" portion of the personal study. If so, how did it go? Take a minute to share.

READ [15 minutes]

Ask someone to read John 6:1–13 aloud for the group. Try to look at these words with new eyes and an open heart. Then read it again silently, circling or underlining words that stand out to you.

> [1] Some time after this, Jesus crossed to the far shore of the Sea of Galilee (that is, the Sea of Tiberias), [2] and a great crowd of people followed him because they saw the signs he had performed by healing the sick. [3] Then Jesus went up on a mountainside and sat down with his disciples. [4] The Jewish Passover Festival was near.
>
> [5] When Jesus looked up and saw a great crowd coming toward him, he said to Philip, "Where shall we buy bread for these people to eat?" [6] He asked this only to test him, for he already had in mind what he was going to do.
>
> [7] Philip answered him, "It would take more than half a year's wages to buy enough bread for each one to have a bite!"

[8] Another of his disciples, Andrew, Simon Peter's brother, spoke up, [9] "Here is a boy with five small barley loaves and two small fish, but how far will they go among so many?"

[10] Jesus said, "Have the people sit down." There was plenty of grass in that place, and they sat down (about five thousand men were there). [11] Jesus then took the loaves, gave thanks, and distributed to those who were seated as much as they wanted. He did the same with the fish.

[12] When they had all had enough to eat, he said to his disciples, "Gather the pieces that are left over. Let nothing be wasted." [13] So they gathered them and filled twelve baskets with the pieces of the five barley loaves left over by those who had eaten.

Turn to the person next to you and take turns sharing your answers to the following questions:

· What was one thing that stood out to you from the passage?
· Why do these words stand out to you—and what fresh insight do they bring?
· In verse 5, Jesus tested Philip by asking where to buy bread for all the people. What was Jesus testing? Does Jesus still test our hearts today by putting large tasks in front of us? Explain your thoughts.

WATCH [25 minutes]

Now play the video for this session. As you watch, use the following outline to record any key thoughts or concepts that stand out to you.

We can choose to pick up every disappointment, stress, or frustration that is tossed our way, or we can choose to not pick up that garbage in the first place.

We not only have the choice of how we will *perceive* trials, but we also have a choice as to how we will *react* to them.

The Greek word for *gentleness* in Philippians 4:5 describes a temperament that is seasoned and mature. A gentle person is level-headed and reacts to stress with steadiness and fairness.

Contagiously calm people trust that God is always in control and encourage others around them that everything will be okay.

How can we exude gentleness in tough times? By looking at Paul's promise in Philippians 4:5: *"The Lord is near."*

When we believe the lie that God has left us, our loneliness amplifies the problem. That's why we have to clutch the truth of God's nearness with both hands.

In the story of Jesus feeding the five thousand, his disciples never asked him for help. Instead, they decided the problem was too big and told the Creator of the world what to do.

When we face a problem, instead of starting with what *we have*, let's remember what *Jesus has*. He is with us and will give us everything we need to overcome our difficulties.

DISCUSS [40 minutes]

Discuss what you just watched by answering the following questions.

1. Read aloud Exodus 3:7–12. What fear does Moses express to God in verse 11? How does God respond in verse 12?

2. Does God's response answer Moses's question directly, or is there a deeper fear that God is addressing? Explain your response.

3. Have different people in your group read aloud the following passages: Genesis 15:1, Deuteronomy 31:8, Joshua 1:9, and Isaiah 43:2. What is God's promise in each verse? What common theme do you see running through these verses?

4. Again and again throughout his Word, God promises to be with us. Think about a time when God's presence calmed you in the middle of a storm. How did God's presence change you emotionally, spiritually, and/or physically?

5. Paul says the key to finding gentleness is believing that God is near. However, just like Jesus' disciples, we easily forget he is with us and waiting to help us. What are some things that prevent you from not only knowing but also believing God is near?

6. Have three group members read passages aloud: Galatians 5:22–25, Philippians 2:13, and 2 Peter 1:3. What promise is given in each of these verses?

7. Jesus tells us there will always be troubles in life. But we have the choice to respond to those troubles with gentleness or with frustration. Considering the biblical promises you just read, what specific steps can you take to respond calmly instead of react sharply when anxieties weigh heavily on your shoulders?

8. In John 16:33, Jesus says, "Take heart! I have overcome the world." How did Jesus overcome the entire world? What has Jesus overcome in your personal world?

RESPOND [15 minutes]

(For this activity, each participant will need his or her phone or a sticky note.) In today's session, you saw how your reaction to worry can be so deeply engrained within you that it might take time to retrain your mind and attitudes. To help you do this, set a daily reminder on your phone—something as simple as "God is with me," or a promise from Scripture such as Philippians 4:5, "The Lord is near." Or, if you prefer, write down a Bible verse about God's presence on a sticky note and place it somewhere you'll see it frequently. The goal is to find any way to daily remind yourself that God is near. When your group reconvenes next week, you will talk about the reminders you set and whether or not they helped you face your day differently.

PRAY [15 minutes]

Wrap up this time by talking to your heavenly Father. Your group may want to begin the prayer time by reading aloud these comforting words from Isaiah 41:10:

> So do not fear, for I am with you; do not be dismayed, for I am your God. I will strengthen you and help you; I will uphold you with my righteous right hand.

Now pray for one another. Split up into groups of two or three or circle up and pray for the person next to you. Here are a few suggestions of ways to pray:

- Confess a trial you tend to react to with fear or frustration. Pray specifically that God's fruit of gentleness will overcome this negative tendency.
- Ask God to help you remember his nearness and to squelch the enemy's lie that he has forsaken you.
- Use the Isaiah passage you just read to declare its promises and/or truth over the person you are praying for. (You can insert the person's name into the verse or simply ask that the truth of this verse would be true in his or her life.)

PERSONAL STUDY

Reflect on the content you've covered this week in *Anxious for Nothing* by engaging in any or all of the following C.A.L.M. personal study activities. The time you invest will be well spent, so let God use it to draw you closer to him. As you work through the exercises, write down your responses to the questions, as you will be given a few minutes to share your insights at the start of the next session if you are doing this study with others. If you are reading *Anxious for Nothing* alongside this study, first review chapters 4–5 in the book.

CELEBRATE GOD'S GOODNESS

During this week's group time, Max spoke about the constant closeness of God. What a comforting promise! Reinforce this truth by reading the following passages, which reassure you serve a God who goes before you, comes behind you, and stands beside you in every moment of every day. If you are in a setting that lends itself to doing so, feel free to read the verses aloud as a proclamation. Celebrate the truth the Father loves you and is with you!

> [38] For I am convinced that neither death nor life, neither angels nor demons, neither the present nor the future, nor any powers, [39] neither height nor depth, nor anything else in all creation, will be able to separate us from the love of God that is in Christ Jesus our Lord. (Romans 8:38–39)
>
> [16] "And I will ask the Father, and he will give you another advocate to help you and be with you forever—[17] the Spirit of truth. The world cannot accept him, because it neither sees him nor knows him. But you know him, for he lives with you and will be in you." (John 14:16–17)
>
> [7] Where can I go from your Spirit? Where can I flee from your presence? [8] If I go up to the heavens, you are there; if I make my bed in the depths, you are there. [9] If I rise on the wings of the dawn, if I settle on the far side of the sea, [10] even there your hand will guide me, your right hand will hold me fast. (Psalm 139:7–10)

1. In Romans 8:38–39, Paul makes a list of what will never separate us from God. Take a moment to create your own version of this passage by filling in the blanks below. Note any decisions you have made, words you have said, or thoughts you have had that *should* have kept God away—but did not (and never will) keep the Lord from loving you.

For I am convinced that

neither_____

nor_____

neither_____

nor _____

nor _____

. . . nor anything else in all creation, will be able to separate us from the love of God that is in Christ Jesus our Lord.

2. What does the psalmist say about God's presence in Psalm 139:7–10? How do you respond to his statement that there is nowhere you can go that God is not already there?

3. Underline a promise from one of the above verses that particularly encourages you today. Write down why you chose to underline those words. How do they bring you comfort?

PRAY

Thank the Lord for the promise you underlined above. Thank him for being near to you no matter what you do—and no matter if you notice. Then just sit in his presence. Be still and rest in the promise that he is near.

> You will be tempted to press the button and release . . . angry outbursts, a rash of accusations, a fiery retaliation of hurtful words. Unchecked anxiety unleashes an Enola Gay of destruction. How many people have been wounded as a result of unbridled stress? And how many disasters have been averted because one person refused to buckle under the strain? It is this composure Paul is summoning in the first of a triad of proclamations. "Let your gentleness be evident to all. The Lord is near. Do not be anxious about anything" (Philippians 4:5–6).[6]

ASK GOD *for* HELP

The Bible reassures us that God is always near—as near as a family member who lives in the same house is to us. But if we're honest, picturing God as being near is different than picturing another human being close to us. So, before you begin this study, consider whether you have ever doubted God's nearness—whether that is something you felt recently or long ago. Write specifically about a time you thought God was too far away or had forgotten about you.

Now read the following passage from Daniel 2:1–23 and answer the questions that follow.

> [1] In the second year of his reign, Nebuchadnezzar had dreams; his mind was troubled and he could not sleep. [2] So the king summoned the magicians, enchanters, sorcerers and astrologers to tell him what he had dreamed. When they came in and stood before the king, [3] he said to them, "I have had a dream that troubles me and I want to know what it means."
>
> [4] Then the astrologers answered the king, "May the king live forever! Tell your servants the dream, and we will interpret it."
>
> [5] The king replied to the astrologers, "This is what I have firmly decided: If you do not tell me what my dream was and interpret it, I will have you cut into pieces and your houses turned into piles of rubble. [6] But if you tell me the dream and explain it, you will receive from me gifts and rewards and great honor. So tell me the dream and interpret it for me."
>
> [7] Once more they replied, "Let the king tell his servants the dream, and we will interpret it."
>
> [8] Then the king answered, "I am certain that you are trying to gain time, because you realize that this is what I have firmly decided: [9] If you

do not tell me the dream, there is only one penalty for you. You have conspired to tell me misleading and wicked things, hoping the situation will change. So then, tell me the dream, and I will know that you can interpret it for me."

[10] The astrologers answered the king, "There is no one on earth who can do what the king asks! No king, however great and mighty, has ever asked such a thing of any magician or enchanter or astrologer. [11] What the king asks is too difficult. No one can reveal it to the king except the gods, and they do not live among humans."

[12] This made the king so angry and furious that he ordered the execution of all the wise men of Babylon. [13] So the decree was issued to put the wise men to death, and men were sent to look for Daniel and his friends to put them to death.

[14] When Arioch, the commander of the king's guard, had gone out to put to death the wise men of Babylon, Daniel spoke to him with wisdom and tact. [15] He asked the king's officer, "Why did the king issue such a harsh decree?" Arioch then explained the matter to Daniel. [16] At this, Daniel went in to the king and asked for time, so that he might interpret the dream for him.

[17] Then Daniel returned to his house and explained the matter to his friends Hananiah, Mishael and Azariah. [18] He urged them to plead for mercy from the God of heaven concerning this mystery, so that he and his friends might not be executed with the rest of the wise men of Babylon. [19] During the night the mystery was revealed to Daniel in a vision. Then Daniel praised the God of heaven [20] and said:

"Praise be to the name of God for ever and ever;
    wisdom and power are his.
[21] He changes times and seasons;
    he deposes kings and raises up others.
He gives wisdom to the wise
    and knowledge to the discerning.
[22] He reveals deep and hidden things;
    he knows what lies in darkness,
    and light dwells with him.

> 23 I thank and praise you, God of my ancestors:
>   You have given me wisdom and power,
> you have made known to me what we asked of you,
>   you have made known to us the dream of the king."

1. What did the king request of the seers? What did he threaten if the request was not fulfilled?

2. How did the astrologers respond to the king's request (see verses 10–11)?

3. The astrologers reacted out of fear and leaned on their own understanding. Who or what do you usually lean on before leaning on the Lord in a stressful situation?

4. How does Daniel's response to the king's request (see verses 16–18) differ from the astrologers'?

5. The astrologers reacted to the unthinkable task, while Daniel responded with gentleness, asking for time and then going to God in prayer. Although you do not have a king threatening your head, life throws a lot of requests and problems your way. What do you learn from Daniel's response about how to handle those demands? How can you follow his example in everyday life?

6. What promise can you take away from Daniel's worship of God in verse 23?

PRAY

No matter what worrisome task you're facing, God is always near to give you wisdom in every situation, just as he gave to Daniel. You only need to ask. What a gift! Conclude your time by asking for a heart like Daniel's—one that is quick to turn to the Lord for wisdom in every circumstance. Review Daniel's proclamation in verses 20–23, soaking in those beautiful words. Thank the Lord for making his power and wisdom available in your life.

> Do not assume God is watching from a distance. Avoid the quicksand that bears the marker "God has left you!" Do not indulge this lie. If you do, your problem will be amplified by a sense of loneliness. It's one thing to face a challenge, but to face it all alone? Isolation creates a downward cycle of fret. Choose instead to be the person who clutches the presence of God with both hands. "The LORD is with me; I will not be afraid. What can mere mortals do to me?" (Psalm 118:6). Because the Lord is near, we can be anxious for nothing.[7]

LEAVE YOUR CONCERNS *with* GOD

In this session, we have been studying God's nearness. Because he is near, there is no reason for us to be anxious. Because he is near, we can face every worry with gentleness. What specific anxieties are weighing on you today? Write each worry in the left column below. When you are finished, ask the Lord how you might demonstrate calmness in each of the struggles you listed. Record your thoughts in the right column next to each worry you wrote.

WORRIES	HOW I CAN FACE IT WITH CALMNESS

TAKE ACTION!

What does an average weekday look like for you? In the space below, briefly list your typical schedule. (If you don't have a typical schedule, just use today as your example.)

Morning:

Afternoon:

Evening:

Focus on the schedule you just jotted down. Line by line, picture God being with you. With you as you grab your coffee. With you as you sit in traffic. With you at your work desk or the kitchen sink. Just with you. How does this mental exercise change the way you view your day and face everyday trials?

PRAY

Ask the Lord to help you sense his presence anytime one of these anxieties threatens your peace. Lay each worry at his feet, remembering he is with you. Thank him for being there even when you don't acknowledge him in the busyness of life.

> Instead of starting with what you have, start with Jesus. Start with his wealth, his resources, and his strength. Before you open the ledger, open your heart. Before you count coins or count heads, count the number of times Jesus has helped you face the impossible. . . . Present the challenge to your Father and ask for help. Will he solve the issue? Yes, he will. Will he solve it immediately? Maybe. Or maybe part of the test is an advanced course in patience. This much is sure: Contagious calm will happen to the degree that we turn to him.[8]

MEDITATE *on* GOOD THINGS

Open your Bible and study Philippians 4:5—"Let your gentleness be evident to all. The Lord is near"—until you can recite it from memory. Don't forget to memorize the verse reference as well. After you've reviewed this verse several times, write down Philippians 4:4 (the verse you memorized last week) and this verse in the space below.

Philippians 4:4

Philippians 4:5

Close by asking the Lord to bring these verses to mind any time an anxious thought surfaces.

CATCH UP *and* READ AHEAD

Use this time to go back and complete any of the study and reflection questions from previous studies that you weren't able to finish. Make a note below of any questions you've had and reflect on any growth or personal insights you've gained.

Read chapters 6–7 in *Anxious for Nothing* before the next group gathering. Use the space below to make note of anything in those chapters that stands out to you or encourages you.

WEEK 3

BEFORE GROUP MEETING	Read chapters 6–7 in *Anxious for Nothing* Read the Welcome section (page 52)
GROUP MEETING	Discuss the Connect questions Read the passage for this session and discuss Watch the video teaching for session 3 Discuss the questions that follow as a group Do the closing exercise and pray (pages 53–60)
STUDY 1	Complete the personal study (pages 62–63)
STUDY 2	Complete the personal study (pages 64–68)
STUDY 3	Complete the personal study (pages 69–71)
STUDY 4	Complete the personal study (page 72)
CATCH UP AND READ AHEAD (BEFORE WEEK 4 GROUP MEETING)	Read chapter 8 in *Anxious for Nothing* Complete any unfinished personal studies (page 73)

PRESENT YOUR REQUESTS *to* GOD

The power of prayer is not in chanting the right formula or quoting some secret code but in the heart of the one praying. God is not manipulated or impressed by formulas or eloquence, but he is moved by sincere requests. As his children, we honor him when we tell him exactly what we need.

MAX LUCADO

WELCOME [read on your own]

"In *every* situation, by prayer and petition, with thanksgiving, present your requests to God" (Philippians 4:6, emphasis added).

Really? In *every* situation pray with thanksgiving?

Even when that punk takes your parking spot? Even when there is no more creamer in the fridge, your toddler is screaming bloody murder, and all you want is a cup of coffee?

Even when she says, "I have cancer," or he leaves after decades of marriage?

Surely not! Surely the original Greek translation of this verse means "in *most* situations pray with thanksgiving."

In her book *The Hiding Place*, Corrie ten Boom tells a remarkable story about gratitude. During World War II, she and her sister Betsie lived in three different concentration camps. The entire ten Boom family had been arrested for providing a safe haven to Jews and Nazi rebels. It's estimated they saved eight hundred lives before being caught and sent away.

Corrie describes how the barracks of the Ravensbruck concentration camp in Germany was infested with fleas. The sisters were forced to sleep on wooden platforms with straw on top, but the straw was dirty, smelly, and crawling with the skin-biting pests. Corrie writes:

> I sat up quickly and bumped my head on the platform above. "Fleas!" I jumped down to the floor. "The place is crawling with fleas! I . . . I don't know how I can cope with living in such a terrible place!"
>
> "Corrie, I think God has already given us the answer," my sister Betsie said. "What was that verse we read from the Bible this morning?"
>
> I pulled out my Bible from the bag I wore on a string around my neck. In the dim light, I read from 1 Thessalonians 5:16–18: "'Rejoice evermore. Pray without ceasing. In every thing give thanks: for this is the will of God in Christ Jesus concerning you.' Oh, Betsie, that's too hard in a place like this!"
>
> "No, come on, Corrie—let's try. What are we thankful for?" my sister asked.
>
> "Well . . . if we must be in this awful place, I'm thankful that we're together." . . .
>
> "That's right!" Betsie's eyes danced. "And thank you, God, for the fleas—"[9]

Corrie goes on to say that the flea infestation kept the guards out of their barracks, allowing Corrie and Betsie to read the Bible aloud twice a day for any woman who wanted to hear. More and more women found the light of Christ in the darkest of places because of *fleas*. Yes, there is a reason to be grateful in *every* circumstance.

CONNECT [10 minutes]

Get this session started by choosing one or both of the following questions to discuss together as a group:

· Corrie ten Boom famously asked the question, "Is prayer your steering wheel or your spare tire?" What do you think this question means? How would you personally answer it?

—*or*—

· How does a grateful heart affect your attitude toward anxiety? Share a time when choosing gratitude changed the way you viewed a difficult situation.

If time permits, discuss the following questions related to the last session:

· Last time, we discussed how we need to let our gentleness be made known to all. During the group activity, you set an alarm to daily remind you of God's presence. If you followed through with this daily reminder, share how it encouraged you. How did it bring more calmness to your day or change the way you faced your anxieties?
· If you participated in the C.A.L.M. personal study, what were some things you learned about yourself? Maybe you engaged in the "Take Action!" portion of the personal study. If so, how did it go? Take a minute to share.

READ [15 minutes]

Ask someone to read James 5:13–16 aloud for the group. Try to look at these words with new eyes and an open heart. Then read it again silently, circling or underlining words that stand out to you.

> ¹³ Is anyone among you in trouble? Let them pray. Is anyone happy? Let them sing songs of praise. ¹⁴ Is anyone among you sick? Let them call the elders of the church to pray over them and anoint them with oil in the name of the Lord. ¹⁵ And the prayer offered in faith will make the sick person well; the Lord will raise them up. If they have sinned, they will be forgiven. ¹⁶ Therefore confess your sins to each other and pray for each other so that you may be healed. The prayer of a righteous person is powerful and effective.

Turn to the person next to you and take turns sharing your answers to the following questions:

· What was one thing that stood out to you from the passage?
· Why do these words stand out to you—and what fresh insight do they bring?
· James says the prayers of a righteous person are powerful and effective. When you pray, do you believe your words are powerful and effective? Or do you struggle with believing they make a difference? What is a stumbling block to believing your prayers are powerful?

WATCH [25 minutes]

Now play the video for this session. As you watch, use the following outline to record any key thoughts or concepts that stand out to you.

Our primary call to action in the fight against anxiety is *prayer*.

When Paul calls us to pray in Philippians 4:6, he uses the words prayer, supplication, and request. The words are similar, but not the same. Prayer is a devotion to God. Supplication is humility toward God. A request is a simple petition to God.

In Matthew 14:22–36, we see that as long as Peter kept his eyes on Jesus, he did the impossible . . . but as soon as he looked at the waves, he began to sink. When we shift our eyes off of Christ and onto our anxieties, we, like Peter, begin to drown in worry or despair.

Peter's prayer to Jesus wasn't eloquent (see verse 30). It was simple and specific. God cares more about the heart behind our prayers than the words we use in our prayers.

There are three reasons it's important to be specific with our requests to God: (1) a specific prayer is a serious prayer, (2) a specific prayer opens the door to seeing God at work, and (3) specific prayers create a lighter load.

Paul also calls us to pray with gratitude in Philippians 4:6. Gratitude is a mindful awareness of the benefits God has provided to us in life.

Christ-based contentment is the key to finding joy. Since no one can take our Christ away, no one can take away our joy.

What we have in Christ is greater than anything we don't have in life.

DISCUSS [40 minutes]

Discuss what you just watched by answering the following questions.

1. Read aloud the beginning of the story of Peter walking on the water in Matthew 14:22–24. What was Jesus doing while the disciples were gone (see verse 23)? What does this verse teach about the importance of prayer?

2. Peter's prayer to Jesus as the waves tossed the boat was not eloquent. It was simple, direct, even desperate. Read Luke 18:9–14. According to this parable, what kind of prayer is heart-honoring to God?

3. In the teaching, Max stressed the importance of being specific with our requests to God. When you pray, do you tend to be detailed or vague? Why do you think you have this tendency?

4. Read the following passages aloud: Matthew 7:7–8, John 14:13–14, and Psalm 91:14–16. What is the promise of prayer in each verse?

5. In Philippians 4:6, Paul tells us to pray "with thanksgiving." Throughout his New Testament letters, he continually lists blessing after blessing God has lavished upon us, giving us reasons to always be thankful. Read the following verses aloud: 1 Corinthians 15:51–56, Ephesians 2:1 7, and 1 John 3:1–2. According to these verses, why can we be thankful in any circumstance?

6. Read Philippians 4:11–13. How does Paul say he is able to find contentment in all things (see verse 13)?

7. What area or circumstance in your life do you find yourself complaining about most?

8. How can you apply Philippians 4:13 to your life so that you, like Paul, can find a reason to be grateful in every circumstance?

RESPOND [15 minutes]

This group activity is simple. Take some time to "count your blessings," focusing your minds on God's good gifts instead of your worries. Have everyone in the group share a particular blessing that God has given to him or her.

PRAY [15 minutes]

End your time together by talking with your heavenly Father. Your group may want to begin the prayer time by reading aloud Psalm 136:1–9 (ESV), a passage about giving thanks to the Lord:

> [1] Give thanks to the LORD, for he is good,
>   for his steadfast love endures forever.
> [2] Give thanks to the God of gods,
>   for his steadfast love endures forever.
> [3] Give thanks to the Lord of lords,
>   for his steadfast love endures forever;
>
> [4] to him who alone does great wonders,
>   for his steadfast love endures forever;
> [5] to him who by understanding made the heavens,
>   for his steadfast love endures forever;
> [6] to him who spread out the earth above the waters,
>   for his steadfast love endures forever;
> [7] to him who made the great lights,
>   for his steadfast love endures forever;
> [8] the sun to rule over the day,
>   for his steadfast love endures forever;
> [9] the moon and stars to rule over the night,
>   for his steadfast love endures forever.

Now take some time to pray for one another, either in groups of two or three or with the person sitting next to you. Here are a few suggestions of ways to pray:

- Share a trying circumstance you are *not* thankful for. Ask the Lord to bring about gratitude and even joy when facing this difficulty.
- Pray about prayer! Confess to the Lord any doubt you have about prayer or any lie you have believed about its lack of importance. Ask God to give you a deeper desire to talk to him, and ask him to show you the power and effectiveness of your prayers.
- Ask the Lord to give you contentment in all circumstances. Thank the Lord for his goodness and the blessings he has generously given.

PERSONAL STUDY

Reflect on the content you've covered this week in *Anxious for Nothing* by engaging in any or all of the following C.A.L.M. personal study activities. The time you invest will be well spent, so let God use it to draw you closer to him. As you work through the exercises, write down your responses to the questions, as you will be given a few minutes to share your insights at the start of the next session if you are doing this study with others. If you are reading *Anxious for Nothing* alongside this study, first review chapters 6–7 in the book.

CELEBRATE GOD'S GOODNESS

During this week's group time, Max focused on presenting our requests to God with thankfulness. Read the following passages about some of the undeserved gifts that God has given to his children. Underline the gifts that he promises you in the verses below.

> And my God will meet all your needs according to the riches of his glory in Christ Jesus. (Philippians 4:19)
>
> The angel of the LORD encamps around those who fear him, and he delivers them. (Psalm 34:7)
>
> "My Father's house has many rooms; if that were not so, would I have told you that I am going there to prepare a place for you?" (John 14:2)
>
> "But the Advocate, the Holy Spirit, whom the Father will send in my name, will teach you all things and will remind you of everything I have said to you." (John 14:26)

1. Consider the gifts you underlined. Which blessing stirs the most gratitude in your heart today? Why that particular blessing?

2. How do you react to Jesus' statement in John 14:2 that he is preparing a place for you in his Father's house? What does it stir in you when you consider that gift?

3. We often forget that talking to the Creator of the universe is an immeasurable privilege. Read Hebrews 4:14–16. Why do we have limitless access to the throne room of God?

PRAY

Close your time by remembering the gift of prayer. Although God is a kind and patient Father who always wants to hear our concerns, dedicate this particular prayer time to pure gratitude, rejoicing in who *he* is. Thank him for what he has given you. Thank him for making a way for his children to personally talk to him anytime, any day, about any problem.

> Gratitude is . . . the greatest of virtues. Studies have linked the emotion with a variety of positive effects. Grateful people tend to be more empathetic and forgiving of others. People who keep a gratitude journal are more likely to have a positive outlook on life. Grateful individuals demonstrate less envy, materialism, and self-centeredness. Gratitude improves self-esteem and enhances relationships, quality of sleep, and longevity. If it came in pill form, gratitude would be deemed the miracle cure. It's no wonder, then, that God's anxiety therapy includes a large, delightful dollop of gratitude.[10]

ASK GOD *for* HELP

God invites us to bring our requests to him. We have the promise that "every good and perfect gift is from above, coming down from the Father of the heavenly lights" (James 1:17). However, our natural human tendency is to try to resolve our problems in our own strength. Take a minute to examine your own heart. When you are facing a problem, what hurdles tend to keep you from taking it to God first? Be specific as you write down your response.

Now read the following passage from Matthew 26:36–46 and answer the questions that follow.

36 Then Jesus went with his disciples to a place called Gethsemane, and he said to them, "Sit here while I go over there and pray." 37 He took Peter and the two sons of Zebedee along with him, and he began to be sorrowful and troubled. 38 Then he said to them, "My soul is overwhelmed with sorrow to the point of death. Stay here and keep watch with me."

39 Going a little farther, he fell with his face to the ground and prayed, "My Father, if it is possible, may this cup be taken from me. Yet not as I will, but as you will."

40 Then he returned to his disciples and found them sleeping. "Couldn't you men keep watch with me for one hour?" he asked Peter. 41 "Watch and pray so that you will not fall into temptation. The spirit is willing, but the flesh is weak."

42 He went away a second time and prayed, "My Father, if it is not possible for this cup to be taken away unless I drink it, may your will be done."

> ⁴³ When he came back, he again found them sleeping, because their eyes were heavy. ⁴⁴ So he left them and went away once more and prayed the third time, saying the same thing.
>
> ⁴⁵ Then he returned to the disciples and said to them, "Are you still sleeping and resting? Look, the hour has come, and the Son of Man is delivered into the hands of sinners. ⁴⁶ Rise! Let us go! Here comes my betrayer!"

1. Jesus set the perfect example of taking every request to God. Again and again in the Gospels, we see him going to a secluded place to pray. Here we see him praying to the Father on the night of his arrest. What was Jesus' posture as he prayed? What does this posture say about his attitude toward the Father?

2. Reread verse 39. What specific words of Jesus prick your heart? Why do these words especially touch you today?

3. After reading Jesus' conversation with the Father—his face in the dirt of the Garden of Gethsemane—what do you think the Lord wants to teach you through Jesus' example? What about Jesus' prayer do you want to incorporate into your own prayer life?

4. What does Jesus tell his disciples to do in verse 41?

Jesus warned his disciples that when it comes to temptation, the spirit is willing but the flesh is weak. When it comes to prayer, isn't the same true? The Holy Spirit within us wants us to remain close to the Father, while our flesh wants to rely on our own strength. Our pride often keeps us from prayer but, as Paul wrote, the Spirit inside of us actually helps us to pray:

> [26] In the same way, the Spirit helps us in our weakness. We do not know what we ought to pray for, but the Spirit himself intercedes for us through wordless groans. [27] And he who searches our hearts knows the mind of the Spirit, because the Spirit intercedes for God's people in accordance with the will of God (Romans 8:26–27).

5. Based on this passage from Romans, what is the Holy Spirit actively doing in you even when you don't know the words to pray?

PRAY

There is a spiritual battle warring over your prayer life, because the enemy knows how powerful prayer is. So today, ask God to help you overcome any fleshly attitude you have toward prayer. Ask him to help you walk in the Spirit, press into prayer, and believe that it has power.

> God doesn't delay. He never places you on hold or tells you to call again later. God loves the sound of your voice. Always. He doesn't hide when you call. He hears your prayers. For that reason, "be anxious for nothing, but in everything by prayer and supplication, with thanksgiving, let your requests be made known to God" (Philippians 4:6 NKJV). With this verse the apostle calls us to take action against anxiety. Until this point he has been assuring us of God's character: his sovereignty, mercy, and presence. Now it is our turn to act on this belief. We choose prayer over despair. Peace happens when people pray.[11]

LEAVE YOUR CONCERNS *with* GOD

Have you ever started a sentence with the phrase "if only"?

If only I could drive a new car instead of this old clunker, then I would be less stressed.

If only I could be married, then I wouldn't feel lonely.

If only I had more money, then I would be happy.

The *if only* syndrome can lead you to conclude that the good life is only one purchase away, one romance away, or one promotion away. It's a lie that can lead you to borrow more money, work long hours, and take unnecessary risks.

The antidote to the *if only* syndrome is gratitude. Why? Because gratitude forces you to recognize what God has *already* given to you. While the anxious heart says, "Lord, if only I had this, that, or the other, I'd be okay . . ." the grateful heart says, "Lord, you've *already* given me this, that, and the other, and I thank you for it."

What are the *if onlys* in your life? Write each *if only* in the left column below. Then practice what we studied in this session—the powerful heart-changing medicine of gratitude—by listing your *alreadys* in the right column. As you do, think about how noting each of these *alreadys* changes your perspective about your first list—the *if onlys*.

IF ONLYS	ALREADYS

TAKE ACTION!

Take this activity a step further by encouraging someone else. Reach out to a person in your life who is an *already*—someone who has already loved you or helped you in the past. Let that person know that you are thankful for him or her today.

PRAY

For this prayer time, use the words of Paul in Philippians 4:12–13. Fill in the blanks with circumstances or desires that have caused you to be ungrateful and anxious.

I know what it is to be in need, and I know what it is to have plenty. I have learned the secret of being content in any and every situation, whether _____ _____ _____ or _____ _____ _____, whether _____ _____ or _____ _____. I can do all this through him who gives me strength.

Leave these circumstances at the feet of your heavenly Father and conclude your prayer time by thanking him for your *alreadys*.

What you have in Christ is greater than anything you don't have in life. You have God, who is crazy about you, and the forces of heaven to monitor and protect you. You have the living presence of Jesus within you. In Christ you have everything he can give you, a happiness that can never be taken, a grace that will never expire, and a wisdom that will ever increase. He is a fountain of living hope that will never be exhausted.[12]

MEDITATE *on* GOOD THINGS

Open your Bible and study Philippians 4:6—"But in every situation, by prayer and petition, with thanksgiving, present your requests to God"—until you can recite it from memory. Don't forget to memorize the verse reference as well. After you've reviewed this verse several times, write down Philippians 4:4 (the verse you memorized in week one), Philippians 4:5 (the verse you memorized in week two), and this verse in the space below.

Philippians 4:4

Philippians 4:5

Philippians 4:6

Close by asking the Lord to bring these verses to mind any time an anxious thought surfaces.

CATCH UP *and* READ AHEAD

Use this time to go back and complete any of the study and reflection questions from previous studies that you weren't able to finish. Make a note below of any questions you've had and reflect on any growth or personal insights you've gained.

Read chapter 8 in *Anxious for Nothing* before the next group gathering. Use the space below to make note of anything in those chapters that stands out to you or encourages you.

WEEK 4

BEFORE GROUP MEETING	Read chapter 8 in *Anxious for Nothing* Read the Welcome section (page 76)
GROUP MEETING	Discuss the Connect questions Read the passage for this session and discuss Watch the video teaching for session 4 Discuss the questions that follow as a group Do the closing exercise and pray (pages 77-84)
STUDY 1	Complete the personal study (pages 86-88)
STUDY 2	Complete the personal study (pages 89-94)
STUDY 3	Complete the personal study (pages 95-97)
STUDY 4	Complete the personal study (page 98)
CATCH UP AND READ AHEAD (BEFORE WEEK 5 GROUP MEETING)	Read chapters 9-11 in *Anxious for Nothing* Complete any unfinished personal studies (page 99)

THE PEACE *of* GOD *will* GUARD YOUR HEART

Our Father gives us the very peace of God.
He downloads the tranquility of the throne room into
our world, resulting in an inexplicable calm.
We should be worried, but we aren't. We should
be upset, but we are comforted. The peace of God
transcends all logic, scheming, and efforts to explain it.

MAX LUCADO

WELCOME [read on your own]

When strolling the streets of Istanbul, Turkey, there is no sight more majestic than the Hagia Sophia. Its central dome, standing 105 feet tall and surrounded by four pencil-shaped minarets stretching more than 200 feet into the heavens, can be spotted from miles away. The dome often serves as a "north star" for lost tourists.

In AD 532, Emperor Justinian I made the Hagia Sophia what it is today. It served as a Christian cathedral for more than a millennium, until AD 1453. That year, the Ottoman Empire took over Constantinople (modern-day Istanbul) and declared the Hagia Sophia to be a mosque. Today, it is a museum.

When I (Jenna) stepped into the Hagia Sophia, I could immediately see the layers of history within its walls. Much restoration and repair have peeled back the yellow paint the Ottomans used to cover up Christian symbols and mosaics. One particular mosaic that caught my attention stood over the Imperial Door, which was used only by the emperors.

The mosaic depicts Jesus sitting on a throne of jewels. Some people are around him, but I didn't pay much attention to them. My focus was drawn to his hands. Jesus is holding what looks like an open scroll or book. I couldn't read the words, but after doing a little research I learned they say, "Peace be with you. I am the light of the world."

Peace be with you.

Written high over the twenty-three-foot-tall oak doors are the words, "Peace be with you." Written above the doors that more than three million tourists walk through a year are the words, "Peace be with you." Written above the doors that welcomed emperors who worshiped themselves and sultans who prayed to a different god are the words, "Peace be with you."

I wonder how many people over the centuries have actually looked at those words and received the invitation. *Peace.* Not just any peace. God's peace. A peace that surpasses all understanding. And just as this peace frames the doorway of the Hagia Sophia, so it frames our hearts if we will allow it. It's a peace that guards our hearts and minds in Christ.

This peace is a constant invitation in our lives as we walk through the doors of decisions, of relationships, of daily tasks. But how many times do we stop to accept it?

"And the peace of God, which transcends all understanding, will guard your hearts and your minds in Christ Jesus" (Philippians 4:7). Today, let's look up and say yes to the invitation of this beautiful promise.

CONNECT [10 minutes]

Get this session started by choosing one or both of the following questions to discuss together as a group:

· Have you ever endured a torrential (physical) storm? Describe the fierceness of the storm and how you withstood its strength.

—or—

· Have you ever endured a perfect storm of bad events? What happened? How did you spiritually and emotionally face the storm?

If time permits, discuss the following questions related to the last session:

· Last time, we discussed leaving our requests with God. How has this truth brought you more peace since the last time we met?
· If you participated in the C.A.L.M. personal study, what were some things you learned about yourself? Maybe you engaged in the "Take Action!" portion of the personal study. If so, how did it go? Take a minute to share.

READ [15 minutes]

Ask someone to read aloud 2 Chronicles 20:1–12 for the group. Try to look at these words with new eyes and an open heart. Then read it again silently, circling or underlining words that stand out to you.

> [1] After this, the Moabites and Ammonites with some of the Meunites came to wage war against Jehoshaphat.
> [2] Some people came and told Jehoshaphat, "A vast army is coming against you from Edom, from the other side of the Dead Sea. It is already in Hazezon Tamar" (that is, En Gedi). [3] Alarmed, Jehoshaphat resolved to inquire of the LORD, and he proclaimed a fast for all Judah. [4] The people of Judah came together to seek help from the LORD; indeed, they came from every town in Judah to seek him.

⁵ Then Jehoshaphat stood up in the assembly of Judah and Jerusalem at the temple of the Lᴏʀᴅ in the front of the new courtyard ⁶ and said:

"Lᴏʀᴅ, the God of our ancestors, are you not the God who is in heaven? You rule over all the kingdoms of the nations. Power and might are in your hand, and no one can withstand you. ⁷ Our God, did you not drive out the inhabitants of this land before your people Israel and give it forever to the descendants of Abraham your friend? ⁸ They have lived in it and have built in it a sanctuary for your Name, saying, ⁹ 'If calamity comes upon us, whether the sword of judgment, or plague or famine, we will stand in your presence before this temple that bears your Name and will cry out to you in our distress, and you will hear us and save us.'

¹⁰ "But now here are men from Ammon, Moab and Mount Seir, whose territory you would not allow Israel to invade when they came from Egypt; so they turned away from them and did not destroy them. ¹¹ See how they are repaying us by coming to drive us out of the possession you gave us as an inheritance. ¹² Our God, will you not judge them? For we have no power to face this vast army that is attacking us. We do not know what to do, but our eyes are on you."

Turn to the person next to you and take turns sharing your answers to the following questions:

· What was one thing that stood out to you from the passage?
· Why do these words stand out to you—and what fresh insight do they bring?
· What was Jehoshaphat's response to the perfect storm of armies that were preparing to attack (see verses 3 and 12)? When the perfect storm of anxiety is looming in your own life, how can you respond like Jehoshaphat?

WATCH [25 minutes]

Now play the video for this session. As you watch, use the following outline to record any key thoughts or concepts that stand out to you.

"Where is God?" is one of the first and most common questions we ask when facing life's storms.

The disciples must have asked this question as they were tossed about by the Sea of Galilee, no Jesus in sight, alone in the storm for nine hours.

When we face the tempestuous storms of life, Paul encourages us with these words from Philippians 4:7: "And the peace of God, which surpasses all understanding, will guard your hearts and minds in Christ Jesus" (ESV).

As we do our part—rejoice in the Lord, pursue a gentle spirit, pray about everything, and cling to gratitude—God does his part. He bestows on us the peace of God.

This peace of God that Paul promises is not just from God, it's of God.

As we rejoice in God, continue to pray, and cast our worries on him, he builds a fortress of peace around our hearts and our minds.

When Paul and his fellow shipmates were tossed at sea for fourteen days, an angel of the Lord appeared to Paul and gave him three promises we can hold onto in the storm:

We are not alone. God sends his heavenly helpers to guard us.

We belong to God. Heaven has a place for us.

We are in the Lord's service. God will never let you live one day short of the mission he has given you.

God never promised a life without storms. But he promised to be with us when we face them.

DISCUSS [40 minutes]

Discuss what you just watched by answering the following questions.

1. Read John 14:27 aloud. What is the difference between the "peace" the world gives and the peace God gives?

2. God never promises we will live a storm-free existence. The Bible is full of stories about storms and how to face them. Take a moment to read Matthew 8:23–27. What is Jesus doing during the storm? What is his response to his disciples' fear (see verse 26)?

3. In Matthew 8:26, Jesus says to his disciples, "You of little faith, why are you so afraid?" After saying this, Jesus "got up and rebuked the winds and the waves, and it was completely calm." Could Jesus be telling you the same thing today? What area of your life is dominated too much by fear and not enough by faith?

4. Read Psalm 119:75 and Hebrews 12:6, 11. Many times, the "winds and waves" in our storm are caused by our own poor decisions. And the Lord, just as he rebuked the winds and waves in Galilee, rebukes us for disobeying his Word. According to the verses you just read, why does God discipline us? How can God's rebuke bring calm to our storm?

5. Paul told his shipmates, "Last night an angel of the God to whom I belong and whom I serve stood beside me" (Acts 27:23). There are three promises you can gain from these words. The first promise is that *God will send his angels to help you during life's storms*. Read Psalm 91:11–12, Matthew 18:10, and Hebrews 1:14. What is the promise of each of these verses? How do these verses bring you peace?

6. The second promise is that *you belong to God*. Paul describes God as the One "to whom I belong." Read Psalm 100:3, Isaiah 43:1, and 1 John 3:1. What is the key promise of each of these verses? How could remembering this promise bring you comfort when you consider the storms of life?

7. The final promise is that *God has a heavenly mission for your life.* Read Matthew 22:37–39, 28:19, John 15:16, and Ephesians 2:10. According to these verses, what has God called you to do?

8. In the verses you just read, the heavenly assignments were broader in nature, but God puts specific assignments on our hearts as well. What specific ministry has God assigned to you during this season of life?

RESPOND [15 minutes]

(For this activity, you will need your phone, laptop, or any device containing speakers, along with access to the hymn "It Is Well with My Soul.") God promises to guard our hearts and our minds in Christ Jesus. When we bring our requests before Christ, entrusting our cares into his hands, he serves as a strong wall of protection around our thoughts and our emotions. He gives us a peace we can't comprehend, no matter how big the storm. To meditate on the promise of this peace, play the old and beloved hymn "It Is Well with My Soul." Soak in the words. Sing along if you wish. Pull up the lyrics on your phone if you want to read along. However you choose to listen, allow the promise of these words to bring you deep peace.

PRAY [15 minutes]

Wrap up this time by talking to your heavenly Father. Your group may want to begin the prayer time by reading aloud these comforting words from Psalm 29:10–11:

> [10] The LORD sits enthroned over the flood;
>   the LORD is enthroned as King forever.
> [11] The LORD gives strength to his people;
>   the LORD blesses his people with peace.

Now take some time to pray for one another, either in groups of two or three or with the person sitting next to you. Here are a few suggestions of ways to pray:

· Share an area in your life where God's peace feels faint. Then take turns asking for God's peace to fill the heart of one of your fellow group members.
· Thank God for his peace. Thank him for the promises you discussed today—that he sends his angels regarding you, that you belong to him, and that he is sovereign over your calling in this life.
· Use the passage you just read and declare its promises and/or truth over the person you are praying for. (You can insert the person's name into the verse or simply ask that the truth of this verse would be true in his or her life.)

PERSONAL STUDY

Reflect on the content you've covered this week in *Anxious for Nothing* by engaging in any or all of the following C.A.L.M. personal study activities. The time you invest will be well spent, so let God use it to draw you closer to him. As you work through the exercises, write down your responses to the questions, as you will be given a few minutes to share your insights at the start of the next session if you are doing this study with others. If you are reading *Anxious for Nothing* alongside this study, first review chapter 8 in the book.

CELEBRATE GOD'S GOODNESS

During this week's group time, Max reminded us about the supernatural peace of God. The Lord doesn't just promise us any peace, but *his* peace! What a gift! Read the following passages about this peace that God uses to guard our hearts and minds in him. If you are in a setting that lends itself to doing so, feel free to read the verses aloud as a proclamation. Celebrate the truth that the Prince of Peace is in you and filling you with his peace that surpasses all understanding.

> You will keep in perfect peace those whose minds are steadfast, because they trust in you. (Isaiah 26:3)
>
> 22 But the fruit of the Spirit is love, joy, peace, forbearance, kindness, goodness, faithfulness, 23 gentleness and self-control. Against such things there is no law. 24 Those who belong to Christ Jesus have crucified the flesh with its passions and desires. 25 Since we live by the Spirit, let us keep in step with the Spirit. (Galatians 5:22–25)
>
> Great peace have those who love your law, and nothing can make them stumble. (Psalm 119:165)
>
> For to us a child is born, to us a son is given, and the government will be on his shoulders. And he will be called Wonderful Counselor, Mighty God, Everlasting Father, Prince of Peace. (Isaiah 9:6)

1. Reread the passages and underline the promise in each verse. What particular promise brings you the most comfort today? Why does that promise speak so personally to you?

2. What does the prophet Isaiah say is the key to receiving God's perfect peace (see Isaiah 26:3)? Why do you think trust in God leads to peace in your life?

3. What is significant about the fact that one of the names Isaiah gives to Jesus is "Prince of Peace"? What does that say about God's desire for you to have his peace?

PRAY

For this prayer time, write a thank-you note to God. You can thank him for anything, but if you need suggestions, here are some ideas:

- Thank him for his peace that dwells in you because he himself dwells in you.
- Thank God for the particular promise that encouraged you today.
- Thank him for the refreshing promises of Philippians 4:4–8 and for all he has been teaching you through this study.

As we do our part (rejoice in the Lord, pursue a gentle spirit, pray about everything, and cling to gratitude), God does his part. He bestows upon us the peace of God. Note, this is not a peace from God. Our Father gives us the very peace of God. He downloads the tranquility of the throne room into our world, resulting in an inexplicable calm. We should be worried, but we aren't. We should be upset, but we are comforted. The peace of God transcends all logic, scheming, and efforts to explain it.[13]

ASK GOD *for* HELP

Jesus promises to give us a peace that comes directly from him and surpasses anything we can ever comprehend. Unfortunately, at times we try to find peace in what the world has to offer instead of what God has promised. Think about when you have found this to be true in your life. What was it that led you to seek the world's peace rather than God's peace?

Now read the following story found in 1 Samuel 15:1–26 and answer the questions that follow.

¹ Samuel said to Saul, "I am the one the LORD sent to anoint you king over his people Israel; so listen now to the message from the LORD. ² This is what the LORD Almighty says: 'I will punish the Amalekites for what they did to Israel when they waylaid them as they came up from Egypt. ³ Now go, attack the Amalekites and totally destroy all that belongs to them. Do not spare them; put to death men and women, children and infants, cattle and sheep, camels and donkeys.'"

⁴ So Saul summoned the men and mustered them at Telaim—two hundred thousand foot soldiers and ten thousand from Judah. ⁵ Saul went to the city of Amalek and set an ambush in the ravine. ⁶ Then he said to the Kenites, "Go away, leave the Amalekites so that I do not destroy you along with them; for you showed kindness to all the Israelites when they came up out of Egypt." So the Kenites moved away from the Amalekites.

⁷ Then Saul attacked the Amalekites all the way from Havilah to Shur, near the eastern border of Egypt. ⁸ He took Agag king of the Amalekites alive, and all his people he totally destroyed with the sword. ⁹ But Saul

and the army spared Agag and the best of the sheep and cattle, the fat calves and lambs—everything that was good. These they were unwilling to destroy completely, but everything that was despised and weak they totally destroyed.

[10] Then the word of the LORD came to Samuel: [11] "I regret that I have made Saul king, because he has turned away from me and has not carried out my instructions." Samuel was angry, and he cried out to the LORD all that night.

[12] Early in the morning Samuel got up and went to meet Saul, but he was told, "Saul has gone to Carmel. There he has set up a monument in his own honor and has turned and gone on down to Gilgal."

[13] When Samuel reached him, Saul said, "The LORD bless you! I have carried out the LORD's instructions."

[14] But Samuel said, "What then is this bleating of sheep in my ears? What is this lowing of cattle that I hear?"

[15] Saul answered, "The soldiers brought them from the Amalekites; they spared the best of the sheep and cattle to sacrifice to the LORD your God, but we totally destroyed the rest."

[16] "Enough!" Samuel said to Saul. "Let me tell you what the LORD said to me last night."

"Tell me," Saul replied.

[17] Samuel said, "Although you were once small in your own eyes, did you not become the head of the tribes of Israel? The LORD anointed you king over Israel. [18] And he sent you on a mission, saying, 'Go and completely destroy those wicked people, the Amalekites; wage war against them until you have wiped them out.' [19] Why did you not obey the LORD? Why did you pounce on the plunder and do evil in the eyes of the LORD?"

[20] "But I did obey the LORD," Saul said. "I went on the mission the LORD assigned me. I completely destroyed the Amalekites and brought back Agag their king. [21] The soldiers took sheep and cattle from the plunder, the best of what was devoted to God, in order to sacrifice them to the LORD your God at Gilgal."

[22] But Samuel replied:

"Does the LORD delight in burnt offerings and sacrifices
    as much as in obeying the LORD?

To obey is better than sacrifice,
and to heed is better than the fat of rams.
23 For rebellion is like the sin of divination,
and arrogance like the evil of idolatry.
Because you have rejected the word of the LORD,
he has rejected you as king."

24 Then Saul said to Samuel, "I have sinned. I violated the LORD's command and your instructions. I was afraid of the men and so I gave in to them. 25 Now I beg you, forgive my sin and come back with me, so that I may worship the LORD."

26 But Samuel said to him, "I will not go back with you. You have rejected the word of the LORD, and the LORD has rejected you as king over Israel!"

1. What was God's specific command to Saul in verse 3?

2. How did Saul disobey God's command (see verse 9)?

3. Samuel confronted Saul with God's anger, rebuking him for keeping some of the spoils instead of completely destroying the Amalekites as the Lord had commanded. What was Saul's initial response to this rebuke (see verses 20–21)?

4. Saul finally confessed in verse 24 that he had disobeyed God by fearing the people instead of the Lord and had allowed the Israelites to take desired spoils from the Amalekites. We, like Saul, are often likewise guilty of fearing man more than God. Deep down, we believe that pleasing others will give us the peace our souls long for. What was a time that you decided to please others instead of God, seeking peace in the wrong place?

5. Initially, Saul came to Samuel with a victorious smile. He was at peace because everyone was happy. But this "peace" that came from pleasing the people of Israel soon faded, for it wasn't true peace. It was a façade, a temporary feeling of pleasure. Saul quickly found that pleasing the Lord was the only source of true peace. How have you found this to be true in your life?

We are all guilty of seeking peace in the wrong places. When we do this, we rob God of his promise to guard our hearts and our minds with his peace beyond our understanding.

PRAY

End this time by asking God to help you find peace in him and him alone. Ask the Lord to surface anything or anyone you are leaning on for peace, and then confess those things to him. Ask him to help you turn to him for peace instead of the counterfeit "peace" the world offers.

> When you gave your life to [God], he took responsibility for you. He guarantees your safe arrival into his port. You are his sheep; he is your shepherd. Jesus said, "I am the good shepherd; I know my sheep and my sheep know me" (John 10:14). You are a bride; he is your bridegroom. The church is being "prepared as a bride adorned for her husband" (Revelation 21:2 ESV). You are his child; he is your father. "You are no longer a slave but God's own child. And since you are his child, God has made you his heir" (Galatians 4:7 NLT). You can have peace in the midst of the storm because you are not alone, you belong to God.[14]

LEAVE YOUR CONCERNS *with* GOD

In this session, we have been studying how the Lord promises to guard our hearts and minds in Christ Jesus. Picture him in military uniform, marching around your heart and mind, protecting you from the enemy's schemes and the worries of this world. He builds a fortress of peace around those he loves. When you leave your requests with God, you are, in a sense, handing over the enemy to the Commander.

Alexander Maclaren, an English minister in the 1800s, called this peace that is promised in Philippians 4:7, God's "Warrior Peace." He wrote, "This Divine peace takes upon itself warlike functions, and garrisons the heart and mind . . . however profound and real that Divine peace is, it is to be enjoyed in the midst of warfare."[15]

Though oxymoronic, "Warrior Peace" could not be a better title for what God offers to us. The worries of this world will not stop attacking us, but we have a God who fights for us—who fights for the peace of our hearts. Let's do our part by handing over our worries to the Commander, entrusting our cares into his hands. With this in mind, write down any worries you have today in the left column. Visualize yourself giving these worries over to your Commander, and then, in the right column, write down what peace this would provide in your life.

WORRIES	WHAT PEACE I WOULD GAIN IN GIVING IT TO GOD

TAKE ACTION!

In the space below, draw a square. Inside the square, draw a heart. Now take the worry or worries you listed above and write them down on the outside of the square.

Read this promise from Psalm 18:2:

> The LORD is my rock, my fortress and my deliverer;
>   my God is my rock, in whom I take refuge,
>   my shield and the horn of my salvation, my stronghold.

When you rejoice in the Lord, remember that he is near, and leave your requests at his feet, he sets up walls of protection around you. He guards you in Christ and keeps the worries of this world from setting up camp in your heart and mind. What you drew above is a tiny glimpse of the spiritual battle of supernatural peace for your heart.

PRAY

For this prayer time, meditate on the words of Psalm 18:2. Then take another look at the worries you listed. Ask the Lord for continual protection from these anxieties.

Northeasters bear down on the best of us. Contrary winds. Crashing waves. They come. But Jesus still catches his children. He still extends his arms. He still sends his angels. Because you belong to him, you can have peace in the midst of the storm. The same Jesus who sent the angel to Paul sends this message to you: "When you pass through the waters, I will be with you" (Isaiah 43:2). You may be facing the perfect storm, but Jesus offers the perfect peace.[16]

MEDITATE *on* GOOD THINGS

Open your Bible and study Philippians 4:7—"And the peace of God, which transcends all understanding, will guard your hearts and your minds in Christ Jesus"—until you can recite it from memory. Don't forget to memorize the verse reference as well. After you've reviewed this verse several times, write down Philippians 4:4 (the verse you memorized in week one), Philippians 4:5 (the verse you memorized in week two), Philippians 4:6 (the verse you memorized last week), and then this verse in the space below.

Philippians 4:4

Philippians 4:5

Philippians 4:6

Philippians 4:7

Close by asking the Lord to bring these verses to mind when you need his peace.

CATCH UP *and* READ AHEAD

Use this time to go back and complete any of the study and reflection questions from previous studies that you weren't able to finish. Make a note below of any questions you've had and reflect on any growth or personal insights you've gained.

Read chapters 9–11 in *Anxious for Nothing* before the next group gathering. Use the space below to make note of anything in those chapters that stands out to you or encourages you.

WEEK 5

BEFORE GROUP MEETING	Read chapters 9–11 in *Anxious for Nothing* Read the Welcome section (page 102)
GROUP MEETING	Discuss the Connect questions Read the passage for this session and discuss Watch the video teaching for session 5 Discuss the questions that follow as a group Do the closing exercise and pray (pages 103–109)
STUDY 1	Complete the personal study (pages 112–114)
STUDY 2	Complete the personal study (pages 115–118)
STUDY 3	Complete the personal study (pages 119–120)
STUDY 4	Complete the personal study (pages 121–122)
WRAP IT UP	Connect with someone in your group (page 123) Complete any unfinished personal studies Connect with your group about the next study that you want to go through together

MEDITATE *on* THESE THINGS

Satan loves to fill our minds with comparisons. He wants to fill our heads with a swarm of anxious and negative thoughts. But the good news is that while there are many things in life over which we have no control, we get to choose what we think about. We get to select our own thought patterns.

MAX LUCADO

WELCOME [read on your own]

Martha. She's always had a bad rap. Probably because she stuck her foot in her mouth at times. She was judgmental, demanding, and maybe a little too opinionated.

But Martha had another side. She was a servant and a nurturer, and boy could she throw a dinner party. Everyone in her village of Bethany probably called her the "hostess with the mostest."

Luke's Gospel tells us of one occasion when Martha discovered Jesus was in town. Immediately she opened the front door and welcomed him in for dinner . . . and possibly some stinky, sweaty disciples too.

Soon the aromas of the kitchen filled the entire house. The oven was full, pots were boiling, Martha was chopping, and time was ticking. "Harrumph!" she muttered with tight lips. "If my sister would come in here and help me with all this, maybe dinner would make it to the table before breakfast."

While Martha was stewing, Mary was listening. She had started out across the room from Jesus, but as Jesus spoke, she couldn't stop listening. She inched closer and closer, till she sat at his feet. All her thoughts were fixed on Jesus, while all of Martha's thoughts were "distracted by all the preparations" (Luke 10:40).

Martha finally reached a point where she was boiling hotter than the soup on the stove. She marched into the living room where Jesus was teaching. "Lord," she said, "don't you care that my sister has left me to do the work by myself? Tell her to help me!" (verse 40).

Mary was embarrassed. The disciples were wide-eyed. And the whole room waited to hear what Jesus would say.

"Martha, Martha," the Lord answered, "you are worried and upset about many things, but few things are needed—or indeed only one. Mary has chosen what is better, and it will not be taken away from her" (verses 41–42).

When it comes to our thoughts, we have a choice. We can focus on the worries of this world. Or we can fix our thoughts on the "only one" that will not be taken from us.

"Mary has *chosen* what is better," Jesus said.

Let's do the same. Just as Jesus entered into Martha and Mary's living room, he has entered into our hearts. That means no matter where we are or what trials come our way, we can sit in his presence and fix our thoughts on his truth.

CONNECT [10 minutes]

Get this session started by choosing one or both of the following questions to discuss together as a group:

· We live in a technology-driven society, with phones, laptops, and tablets at our fingertips. How has technology influenced your thought patterns? How have you seen technology fill your mind with anxious thoughts?

  —or—

· Think about a time when what you thought about a particular challenge you were facing was bigger than the challenge itself. What happened?

If time permits, discuss the following questions related to the last session:

· Last time, we discussed the peace of God that surpasses all understanding. How has this truth brought you more peace since the last time we met?
· If you participated in the C.A.L.M. personal study, what were some things you learned about yourself? Maybe you engaged in the "Take Action!" portion of the personal study. If so, how did it go? Take a minute to share.

READ [15 minutes]

Ask someone to read Luke 10:38–42 aloud for the group. Try to look at these words with new eyes and an open heart. Then read it again silently, circling or underlining words that stand out to you.

> [38] As Jesus and his disciples were on their way, he came to a village where a woman named Martha opened her home to him. [39] She had a sister called Mary, who sat at the Lord's feet listening to what he said. [40] But Martha was distracted by all the preparations that had to be made. She came to him and asked, "Lord, don't you care that my sister has left me to do the work by myself? Tell her to help me!"

> [41] "Martha, Martha," the Lord answered, "you are worried and upset about many things, [42] but few things are needed—or indeed only one. Mary has chosen what is better, and it will not be taken away from her."

Turn to the person next to you and take turns sharing your answers to the following questions:

- What was one thing that stood out to you from the passage?
- Why do these words stand out to you—and what fresh insight do they bring?
- Luke tells us that Martha was "distracted" (verse 40). How did her concerns lead her to treat Jesus and her sister? When your mind is fixed on concerns instead of Christ, how does it lead you to mistreat the ones you love?

WATCH [25 minutes]

Now play the video for this session. As you watch, use the following outline to record any key thoughts or concepts that stand out to you.

The enemy is constantly invading our minds with lies—with thoughts that *we're not good enough*, that *no one will ever love us*, or that *everyone is against us*.

Our minds are constantly under attack. The good news is that while there are many things in life over which we have no control, we get to choose what we think about.

We occupy the control tower of our mental airport.

The bleeding woman had every excuse not to go to Jesus. Her disease had made her an outcast. She could have believed in the lies that said she was unfit or too dirty to touch Christ. But instead she chose to believe that she would be healed.

Paul's words in Philippians 4:8 make it clear that the best way to face anxiety in this life is with clear-headed, logical thinking.

When unknowns come our way, instead of responding with anxious thoughts, we need to hand our minds over to Christ. We need to let him control our thoughts with his truth.

The best way we can filter our thoughts is by clinging to Christ, abiding in him. He is the true vine, and as we hold onto him, he will produce fruit in us.

Our goal is not to bear fruit but to stay attached to the vine. We are to make Christ our home and hold onto him.

DISCUSS [40 minutes]

Discuss what you just watched by answering the following questions.

1. Read aloud John 8:44, Ephesians 6:11–12, and 1 Peter 5:8. What do these verses say about our enemy? What is his mission, and why is it important for us to know all we can about him?

2. In *The Message*, Romans 8:6 reads, "Obsession with self in these matters is a dead end; attention to God leads us out into the open, into a spacious, free life." What type of thoughts specifically lead to a "dead end"? What thoughts lead to a "free life"?

3. Read Romans 12:1–2, 2 Corinthians 10:5, and Ephesians 6:14. What do these verses ask us to do so that our thoughts are not dominated by anxiety? What are some ways we can live out these commands in our everyday lives?

4. Read Mark 5:24–29. What thoughts do you think the enemy had planted in the bleeding woman's mind as she jockeyed her way through the crowd to get to Jesus? What lies has the enemy whispered into your heart to keep you from seeking Christ when you, like the bleeding woman, feel physically or spiritually sick?

5. Instead of listening to the enemy, what does the woman say to herself (see verse 28)? How does Jesus reward the bleeding woman's determined faith (see verses 33–34)? What promise can we take away from his response to her?

6. Read aloud Jesus' words in John 15:1–8 (or have a volunteer do so). One of the best ways we can think on things that are true, noble, right, pure, lovely, admirable, and excellent is by attaching ourselves to the One who embodies truth, nobility, righteousness, purity, love, and all things good and excellent. What does it mean to *abide* in Christ?

7. Jesus says, "If you remain in me and I in you, you will bear much fruit" (John 15:5). What are the fruits we produce when we remain in Christ (see Galatians 5:22–23)?

8. Our goal is not to bear fruit but to stay attached to Christ. What is the difference between these two goals?

RESPOND [15 minutes]

(For this activity, each participant will need a pen and his or her sealed envelope from session one.) To conclude your time together, your group leader will distribute the envelopes you sealed at the end of the first session. These envelopes contain the anxieties you were wrestling with at the time. Once you have received your envelope, open it, read the list of worries you wrote down, and then take fifteen minutes to reflect on the following questions. (If you did not submit an envelope the first week, just reflect on the questions that apply to you.)

- Do the burdens you wrote down the first week still burden you, or has God replaced them with his peace? (Be truthful with yourself, and remember it's all right if the anxieties still weigh you down. God is still at work within you and will accomplish his good purposes in his time.)
- What is the most meaningful lesson that God taught you by studying Philippians 4:4–8?
- How have you personally changed after completing this study?
- What are some specific tools you acquired during this study that you hope to continue to use in order to live an anxiety-free life?

If you are comfortable in doing so, share your thoughts with the group about one or more of the reflection questions above.

PRAY [15 minutes]

For this final prayer time, stay together as a group to pray for one another. Have two people agree to start and finish the prayer. In between, anyone is welcome to pray. Here are a few suggestions on how to pray for your friends:

- Pray that the truth of Philippians 4:4–8 will embed in the heart of every person in your group.
- Pray that the group will respond to Paul's call in this passage—rejoicing in the Lord always, remembering God's nearness, letting all their requests be made known to God, and meditating on the goodness and truth of God.
- Pray against the enemy's schemes to rob you of the truth you learned throughout this study.
- Pray that the peace of God will rule over the hearts and minds of each person in your group.

PERSONAL STUDY

Reflect on the content you've covered during this final week in *Anxious for Nothing* by engaging in any or all of the following C.A.L.M. personal study activities. The time you invest will be well spent, so let God use it to draw you closer to him. As you work through the exercises, write down your responses to the questions. If you are reading *Anxious for Nothing* alongside this study, first review chapters 9–11 in the book.

CELEBRATE GOD'S GOODNESS

During this week's group time, Max explored what the Bible has to say about the power of our thoughts. Our thoughts influence everything we do, feel, and believe. If our thoughts are anxious, then our lives will be anxious. But if our thoughts are centered on God's peace, then our lives will be peaceful.

In Philippians 4:8, Paul tells us, "Finally, brothers and sisters, whatever is true, whatever is noble, whatever is right, whatever is pure, whatever is lovely, whatever is admirable—if anything is excellent or praiseworthy—think about such things." Jesus embodies every adjective in this list. He is true, noble, right, pure, lovely, admirable, and so worthy of our praise!

Meditate on the following passages about how wonderful our Savior is. If your setting lends itself to doing so, read them aloud. Proclaim them to the One who is worthy!

> He was oppressed and afflicted, yet he did not open his mouth; he was led like a lamb to the slaughter, and as a sheep before its shearers is silent, so he did not open his mouth. (Isaiah 53:7)
>
> Rejoice greatly, Daughter Zion! Shout, Daughter Jerusalem! See, your king comes to you, righteous and victorious, lowly and riding on a donkey, on a colt, the foal of a donkey. (Zechariah 9:9)
>
> "The Son of Man did not come to be served, but to serve, and to give his life as a ransom for many." (Matthew 20:28)
>
> God made him who had no sin to be sin for us, so that in him we might become the righteousness of God. (2 Corinthians 5:21)

> [11] I saw heaven standing open and there before me was a white horse, whose rider is called Faithful and True. With justice he judges and wages war.... [16] On his robe and on his thigh he has this name written: KING OF KINGS AND LORD OF LORDS. (Revelation 19:11, 16)

1. What do these passages say about Jesus being a servant? What other title is given to Jesus in Revelation 19:11, 16? Why is that title significant?

2. Look back at these passages and underline any descriptions you find of Jesus. Which of these attributes stands out to you the most? Why that attribute?

3. Now do as Paul instructs you to do—"Think on these things." Read over your descriptions about Jesus a few times, stare at the words, and think about his goodness. Which of these attributes of Jesus would you like to have more of in your life? Why those attributes?

PRAY

Thank Jesus for being the essence of all things good. Review Paul's list and ascribe to the Lord every adjective noted in Philippians 4:8, telling him that he is true, noble, and right.

> The wise man urges, "Be careful what you think, because your thoughts run your life" (Proverbs 4:23 NCV). Do you want to be happy tomorrow? Then sow seeds of happiness today. (Count blessings. Memorize Bible verses. Pray. Sing hymns. Spend time with encouraging people.) Do you want to guarantee tomorrow's misery? Then wallow in a mental mud pit of self-pity or guilt or anxiety today. (Assume the worst. Beat yourself up. Rehearse your regrets. Complain to complainers.) Thoughts have consequences. Healing from anxiety requires healthy thinking.[17]

ASK GOD *for* HELP

You have an enemy who is out to poison your mind with negativity, fear, bitterness, anxiety . . . anything that is not of God. No one is immune to his attacks, and you may even succumb to them without realizing it. What does it look like in your life for you to set your mind on what is true, noble, right, pure, lovely, admirable, excellent, and praiseworthy?

Now read the following passage from Matthew 4:1-11 and answer the questions that follow.

> ¹ Then Jesus was led by the Spirit into the wilderness to be tempted by the devil. ² After fasting forty days and forty nights, he was hungry. ³ The tempter came to him and said, "If you are the Son of God, tell these stones to become bread."
>
> ⁴ Jesus answered, "It is written: 'Man shall not live on bread alone, but on every word that comes from the mouth of God.'"
>
> ⁵ Then the devil took him to the holy city and had him stand on the highest point of the temple. ⁶ "If you are the Son of God," he said, "throw yourself down. For it is written:
>
> "'He will command his angels concerning you,
>   and they will lift you up in their hands,
>   so that you will not strike your foot against a stone.'"
>
> ⁷ Jesus answered him, "It is also written: 'Do not put the Lord your God to the test.'"

> ⁸ Again, the devil took him to a very high mountain and showed him all the kingdoms of the world and their splendor. ⁹ "All this I will give you," he said, "if you will bow down and worship me."
>
> ¹⁰ Jesus said to him, "Away from me, Satan! For it is written: 'Worship the Lord your God, and serve him only.'"
>
> ¹¹ Then the devil left him, and angels came and attended him.

1. When did the tempter choose to attack Jesus (see verse 2)? What is the significance behind the enemy's timing?

2. Often, the enemy will attack when you have been weakened by a difficult circumstance, rocky relationship, lack of sleep, or anything else that makes you feel defeated. When was a time you sensed the enemy attack your thoughts during a season of weakness?

3. What were the temptations Satan used in an attempt to lure Christ away from his mission?

4. The enemy is constantly on the prowl. He wants to fill your mind with doubts about your identity in Christ, just as he challenged Jesus with, "If you are really the Son of God . . ." He wants to plant doubts in your mind about God and his plan for your life, just as he tempted Christ to test God's faithfulness by throwing himself from the temple. How did Jesus fight off the temptation of the enemy? What specific weapon did he use?

5. In Ephesians 6:14, Paul writes, "Stand firm then, with the belt of truth buckled around your waist." God's Word is a weapon against the enemy and the key to a mind filled with peace. When you meditate on the Word of God, you are doing what Paul urges you to do in Philippians 4:8: immersing yourself in that which is true and right. Are you aware of the enemy when he is attacking your mind? If not, why do you think that is? If so, how do you counter his attacks?

PRAY

Ask the Lord to help you sense when the enemy is attacking your mind so you don't dwell on his lies. Ask God to help you be diligent in putting on the belt of truth, daily reading his Word so you can recognize and fend off any thoughts that are not of him.

> Christ is our home. He is our place of refuge and security. We are comfortable in his presence, free to be our authentic selves. We know our way around in him. We know his heart and his ways. We rest in him, find our nourishment in him. His roof of grace protects us from storms of guilt. His walls of providence secure us from destructive winds. His fireplace warms us during the lonely winters of life. We linger in the abode of Christ and never leave.[18]

LEAVE YOUR CONCERNS *with* GOD

In this session, we have been studying the importance of our thought patterns. Although there is not much in life we can control, we *can* control our thoughts! In the left column, write down any worries that are on your mind today. Be specific with what is burdening you as you record each one. Next, apply Paul's meditation list in Philippians 4:8 to the worry list you just compiled. In the right column, next to your list of anxieties, list gifts God has given you that are true, noble, right, pure, lovely, admirable, excellent, or worthy of praise.

WORRIES	GIFTS GOD HAS GIVEN ME

TAKE ACTION!

One of the best ways to find peace when life's problems begin to crowd your mind is to step outside. God's creation has a way of bringing perspective. It helps you remember how big God is and the gifts he has given to you. As you look at the stars, the trees, a sunset, a flock of birds, a sparkling lake or river, you are meditating on the things Paul tells you to think about. So why not take some time to do just that? Step outside. Soak in God's creation. And think of David's words in Psalm 8:3–4:

> ³ When I consider your heavens,
>   the work of your fingers,
> the moon and the stars,
>   which you have set in place,
> ⁴ what is mankind that you are mindful of them,
>   human beings that you care for them?

PRAY

Use the words of Psalm 8:3–4 for your prayer today. It may sound something like this: God, who am I that you are mindful of me? But you are. I'm on your mind. You think of me! Would you help me think of you more? All throughout my day, would you plant thoughts of your goodness in my mind so that I can focus more on you and less on the worries of this world? Ask God to retrain your mind so that when anxious thoughts come, you will focus on his goodness, his loveliness, his righteousness, and all that is worthy of praise.

Is God sovereign over your circumstances? Is he mightier than your problem? Does he have answers to your questions? According to the Bible the answer is yes, yes, and yes! "God . . . is the blessed controller of all things, the king over all kings and the master of all masters" (1 Timothy 6:15 PHILLIPS). If he sustains all and controls all, don't you think he has authority over this situation you face?[19]

MEDITATE *on* GOOD THINGS

It's time for your final challenge! Open your Bible and Philippians 4:8—"Finally, brothers and sisters, whatever is true, whatever is noble, whatever is right, whatever is pure, whatever is lovely, whatever is admirable—if anything is excellent or praiseworthy—think about such things"—until you can recite it from memory. Don't forget to memorize the verse reference as well. After you've reviewed this verse several times, write down Philippians 4:4 (the verse you memorized in week one), Philippians 4:5 (the verse you memorized in week two), Philippians 4:6 (the verse you memorized in week three), Philippians 4:7 (the verse you memorized last week) and then—finally!—this verse in the space below.

Philippians 4:4

Philippians 4:5

Philippians 4:6

Philippians 4:7

Philippians 4:8

Close by asking the Lord to bring this entire passage to mind anytime an anxious thought surfaces and you need to refocus your mind on the things of God.

WRAP IT UP

Use this time to go back and complete any of the study and reflection questions from previous days that you weren't able to finish. Make note of what God has revealed to you in these days. Finally, talk with your group about what study you may want to go through next. Put a date on the calendar for when you'll meet next to study God's Word and dive deeper into community.

LEADER'S GUIDE

Thank you for your willingness to lead a group through *Anxious for Nothing*! What you have chosen to do is important, and much good fruit can come from studies like this. The rewards of being a leader are different from those of participating, and we hope that as you lead you will find your own walk with Jesus deepened by the experience.

Anxious for Nothing is a five-session study built around video content and small-group interaction. As the group leader, imagine yourself as the host of a dinner party. Your job is to take care of your guests by managing all the behind-the-scenes details so that as your guests arrive, they can focus on one another and on interaction around the topic.

As the group leader, your role is not to answer all the questions or reteach the content—the video, book, and study guide will do most of that work. Your job is to guide the experience and cultivate your small group into a kind of teaching community. This will make it a place for members to process, question, and reflect—not receive more instruction.

There are several elements in this leader's resource section that will help you as you structure your study and reflection time, so follow along and take advantage of each one.

BEFORE YOU BEGIN

Before your first meeting, make sure the group members have a copy of this study guide. Alternately, you can hand out the study guides at your first meeting and give the members some time to look over the material and ask any preliminary questions. Also, make sure that the group members are aware that they have access to the streaming videos at any time by following the instructions provided with this guide. During your first meeting, ask the members to provide their names, phone numbers, and email addresses so that you can keep in touch with them.

Generally, the ideal size for a group is eight to ten people, which will ensure that everyone has enough time to participate in discussions. If you have more people, break up the main group into smaller subgroups. Encourage those who show up at the first meeting to commit to attending the duration of the study, as this will help the group members get to know one another, create stability for the group, and help you know how best to prepare to lead the participants through the material.

Each session begins with an opening reflection in the Welcome section. The questions that follow in the Connect section serve as icebreakers to get the group members thinking about the topic. In the rest of the study, it's generally not a good idea to have everyone answer every question—a free-flowing discussion is more desirable. But with the icebreaker question, you can go around the circle and ask each person to respond. Encourage shy people to share, but don't force them.

At your first meeting, let the group members know that each session also contains a personal study section that they can use to continue to engage with the content until the next meeting. While doing this section is optional, it will help participants cement the concepts presented during the group study time and help them better understand how humility will help them see God, themselves, and others more accurately.

Let them know that if they choose to do so, they can watch the video for the next session by accessing the streaming code provided with this study guide. Invite them to bring any questions and insights to your next meeting, especially if they had a breakthrough moment or didn't understand something.

PREPARATION FOR EACH SESSION

As the leader, there are a few things you should do to best prepare for each meeting:

- Read through the session. This will help you become more familiar with the content and know how to structure the discussion times.
- Decide how the videos will be used. Determine whether you want the members to watch the videos ahead of time (again, via the streaming access code provided with this study guide) or together as a group.
- Decide which questions you want to discuss. Based on the length of your group discussions, you may not be able to get through all the questions. So look over the discussion questions provided in each session and mark which ones you definitely want to cover.
- Be familiar with the questions you want to discuss. When the group meets, you'll be watching the clock, so make sure you are familiar with the questions you have selected.

· Pray for your group. Pray for your group members and ask God to lead them as they study his Word and listen to his Spirit. In many cases, there will be no one "right" answer to the questions. Answers will vary, especially when the group members are sharing their personal experiences.

STRUCTURING THE DISCUSSION TIME

You will need to determine with your group how long you want your meetings to last so that you can plan your time accordingly. Suggested times for each section have been provided in this study guide, and if you adhere to these times, your group will meet for two hours:

SECTION	TIME
CONNECT (discuss one or more of the opening questions for the session)	10 minutes
READ (read the opening passage and discuss together as a group)	15 minutes
WATCH (watch the teaching material together and take notes)	25 minutes
DISCUSS (discuss the study questions you selected ahead of time)	40 minutes
RESPOND (write down key takeaways)	15 minutes
PRAY (pray together and dismiss)	15 minutes

As the group leader, it is up to you to keep track of the time and to keep things on schedule. You might want to set a timer for each segment so that both you and the group members know when the time is up. (There are some good phone apps for timers that play a gentle chime or other pleasant sound instead of a disruptive noise.) Don't be concerned if group members are quiet or slow to share. People are often quiet when they are pulling together their ideas, and this might be a new experience for some of them. Just ask a question and let it hang in the air until someone shares. You can then say, "Thank you. What about others? What came to you when you watched that portion of the teaching?"

GROUP DYNAMICS

Leading a group through *Anxious for Nothing* will prove to be highly rewarding both to you and your group members. But you still may encounter challenges along the way! Discussions can get off track. Group members may not be sensitive to the needs and ideas of others. Some might worry that they will be expected to talk about matters that make them feel awkward. Others may express comments that result in disagreements.

To help ease this strain on you and the group, consider the following ground rules:

- When someone raises a question or comment that is off the main topic, suggest you deal with it another time, or, if you feel led to go in that direction, let the group know that you will be spending some time discussing it.
- If someone asks a question that you don't know how to answer, admit it and move on. At your discretion, feel free to invite group members to comment on questions that call for personal experience.
- If you find that one or two people are dominating the discussion time, direct a few questions to others in the group. Outside the main group time, ask the more dominating members to help you draw out the quieter ones. Work to make them part of the solution instead of part of the problem.
- When a disagreement occurs, encourage the group members to process the matter in love. Encourage those on opposite sides to restate what they heard the other side say about the matter, and then invite each side to evaluate if that perception is accurate. Lead the group in examining other passages related to the topic and look for common ground.

When any of these issues arise, encourage your group members to follow these words from Scripture: "Love one another" (John 13:34); "If it is possible, as far as it depends on you, live at peace with everyone" (Romans 12:18); "Whatever is true . . . noble . . . right . . . pure . . . lovely . . . if anything is excellent or praiseworthy—think about such things" (Philippians 4:8); and, "Everyone should be quick to listen, slow to speak and slow to become angry" (James 1:19). This will make your group time more rewarding and beneficial for everyone who attends.

Thank you again for your willingness to lead your group. May God reward your efforts and dedication and make your time together in *Anxious for Nothing* fruitful for his kingdom.

NOTES

1. Joel J. Miller, "The Secret Behind the Bible's Most Highlighted Verse," *Theology That Sticks* (blog), August 24, 2015, https://blogs .ancientfaith.com /joeljmiller/bibles-most-highlighted-verse/.
2. Eugene H. Peterson, *Conversations: The Message with Its Translator* (Colorado Springs, CO: NavPress, 2017), 1438.
3. Max Lucado, *Anxious for Nothing*: Finding Calm in a Chaotic World (Nashville, TN: Nelson Books, 2017), 45.
4. Lucado, *Anxious for Nothing*, 24.
5. Lucado, *Anxious for Nothing*, 59.
6. Lucado, *Anxious for Nothing*, 69.
7. Lucado, *Anxious for Nothing*, 70–71.
8. Lucado, *Anxious for Nothing*, 75–76.
9. Corrie ten Boom, John L. Sherrill, Elizabeth Sherrill, and Sam Wellman, *The Hiding Place*: The Triumphant True Story of Corrie Ten Boom (Uhrichsville, OH: Barbour, 1990).
10. Lucado, *Anxious for Nothing*, 94.
11. Lucado, *Anxious for Nothing*, 82.
12. Lucado, *Anxious for Nothing*, 99.
13. Lucado, *Anxious for Nothing*, 103.
14. Lucado, *Anxious for Nothing*, 111.
15. Alexander Maclaren, *Expositions of Holy Scripture* (New York: Hodder & Stoughton, 1900), http://biblehub.com/commentaries/philippians/4-7.htm.
16. Lucado, *Anxious for Nothing*, 114.
17. Lucado, *Anxious for Nothing*, 121.
18. Lucado, *Anxious for Nothing*, 136.
19. Lucado, *Anxious for Nothing*, 147.

ABOUT THE AUTHOR

Since entering the ministry in 1978, Max Lucado has served churches in Miami, Florida; Rio de Janeiro, Brazil; and San Antonio, Texas. He currently serves as the teaching minister of Oak Hills Church in San Antonio. He is the recipient of the 2021 ECPA Pinnacle Award for his outstanding contribution to the publishing industry and society at large. He is America's bestselling inspirational author with more than 150 million products in print.

Visit his website at MaxLucado.com.
Facebook.com/MaxLucado
Instagram.com/MaxLucado
Twitter.com/MaxLucado
Youtube.com/MaxLucado

The Max Lucado Encouraging Word Podcast

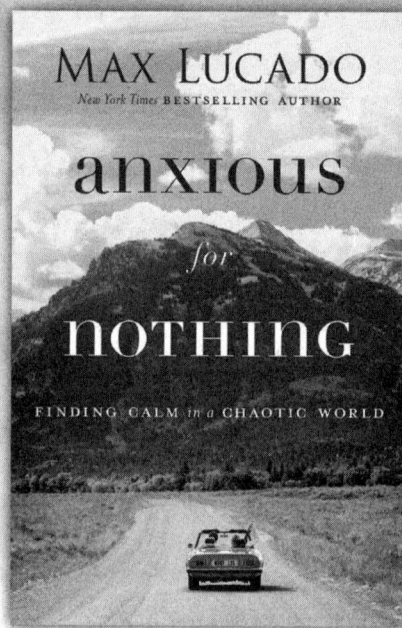